P9-CMA-759

ROCKHURST COLLEGE LIBRARY
0 0006 00954101

A Reference Book of

Property and Liability Reinsurance Management

A REFERENCE BOOK OF

Property and Liability Reinsurance Management

By Robert C. Reinarz, M.B.A.

FOURTH PRINTING, 1979

PUBLISHED BY MISSION PUBLISHING COMPANY
124 WEST WILSHIRE AVENUE, FULLERTON, CALIFORNIA 92632

LIBRARY OF CONGRESS CATALOG CARD NUMBER 68-59174
ISBN 0-916910-01-6
PRINTED IN THE UNITED STATES OF AMERICA

Preface

INSURANCE EXECUTIVES are becoming increasingly aware of the importance of a sound reinsurance program to operating results. Loss and expense ratios are particularly critical today, and reinsurance has a direct effect upon both. As a result, a great deal of care and preparation surrounds the reinsurance purchase. It therefore behooves the persons responsible for this purchase to develop and maintain a high level of knowledge of reinsurance theory and its practice.

Reinsurance is a method of risk handling, nothing more. The insurer's slim profits are realized only through skillful risk assumption and apportionment, where required, through reinsurance. The executive today is pressed by the need to expand with the economy, to provide better service, and, at the same time, to cut expenses to meet competition. A major factor in determing how well he performs this juggling act may just be how conversant he is with reinsurance principles and techniques. This book addresses itself to this end.

The purpose of this book is two-fold. It provides a concise statement of the principles of reinsurance to act as a basis for sound reinsurance decisions. Secondly, it sets out a method of reinsurance programming for use by the reinsurance buyer to act as a basis of reinsurance cost control.

Reinsurance programming, precisely defined, is a method, system, or procedure whereby an optimal arrangement of reinsurance contracts is developed. It is a procedure which enables the insurer to get the most value for his reinsurance cost dollars through a careful evaluation of (1) exposures, (2) size of surplus, (3) premium volume, (4) geographical distribution of premium volume, (5) reinsurance contracts and methods available, and (6) reinsurance costs.

The book is arranged in two parts. Part I, "The Theory and Use of Reinsurance," deals primarily with reinsurance theory, and contains frequent references to practice in order to display specific applications of a principle. For the reader who is well acquainted with reinsurance theory, it is suggested that Part I be lightly skimmed. The index in the back of the book can be used as a guide to Part I on specific points or items of interest.

Part II, "Buying Reinsurance," contains a suggested procedure for establishing a sound reinsurance program. Appendix B, "The Programming Sequence, Statistics, and Exhibits," is included to provide the reinsurance analyst with a guide to the programming process. If followed, the procedure outlined and its exhibits will reveal some interesting facets of the reinsurance program being analyzed.

It is a long and tedious journey one undertakes when he starts to write a book, and without the help of many persons along the way, this one probably would never have been completed. I would like particularly to thank Mr. Ronald C. Comery, Managing Director, Swann and Everett, Ltd., London, England, and Mr. John V. Smith, Corporate Reinsurance Manager, Nationwide Insurance Companies, Columbus, Ohio, for their kind assistance throughout the preparation of the manuscript and for their many suggestions for improvement of Part II.

I would also like to express my thanks to Mr. Brice A. Frey, Jr., Vice President, General Reinsurance Corporation, New York, New York, for his penetrating review of Part II.

A special note of thanks must be tendered to Employers Mutuals of Wausau, Wausau, Wisconsin, for their financial assistance in my research activities and graduate work at the University of Texas, and to Mr. E. R. Sturgeon, Vice President-Reinsurance, at Employers Mutuals for his pains-taking review of the entire manuscript.

Professor John S. Bickley, a fine friend and counselor, has spent many hours working and reworking several sections of the manuscript. His help has immeasurably increased the readability of this book. I shall always remain in his debt for his excellent counsel and patient understanding.

Finally, I must thank my wife, Karen, for her many hours of typing and retyping the manuscript; for her subtle – and unadmitted – changes in the text which smoothed out a multitude of sentences and phrases; for her continued interest in and careful criticism of every section of this book; and finally, for her enduring patience with her husband.

I am most grateful for the help of these specific persons and many more executives and brokers who furnished innumerable points and new ideas.

Regardless of the amount of care that is devoted to the preparation of a book, errors still slip by. For the errors that remain, I claim exclusive credit.

ROBERT C. REINARZ

Los Angeles, California
December 1968

Contents

Tables

Part I

The Theory and Use of Reinsurance

Reinsurance is both a tool for risk sharing and management control. To the knowledgeable, reinsurance offers a unique facility for trimming maximum profits out of the sale of insurance coverages. Part I presents the reader a detailed examination of reinsurance theory as it applies to the various clauses within a contract or reinsurance. Reinsurance underwriting considerations are also included in the examination of the types of reinsurance agreements available and their uses.

CHAPTER I

Reinsurance and its Functions

THE successful reinsurance relationship is one of utmost good faith. It is a transaction between gentlemen of good intent and honest endeavor, both parties realizing that each must find the contract profitable. Utmost good faith (*uberrimae fidei*) is the heart of reinsurance, without which the contract cannot exist, for the reinsurance agreement is a living document. If it is properly adapted, the reinsurer will share both the loss burden and the profits with the primary insurer. This "sharing-of-the-fortunes" of the primary insurer by the reinsurer is what reinsurance is all about. The purpose of this chapter is to provide the reader with a few guide posts to assist in the development of an understanding of the functions of reinsurance and why the tennants of *uberrimae fidei* and share-the-fortunes are the two cardinal rules of reinsurance.

Because of its international character and loose regulation by government bodies, reinsurance has not developed a tight set of definitions upon which all persons can agree. Thus, the *intent* of the reinsurance agreement is given precedence over the exact wording of the contract. The intent is the same from one agreement to the next: the reinsurer is to follow-the-fortunes of the primary insurer. All interpretations of the agreement during its lifetime must have this as a base. It is not sufficient that only the few persons involved in the contract negotiations be aware of this principle. Any person who will be involved in the act of reinsuring under the agreement must also understand. The intent of the agreement is for the reinsurer to enjoy the fruits of the profitable insurance transaction on the part of the primary insurer as well as its share of high hazard, accommodation transactions. In the long run, both must make a profit.

SOME GENERAL DEFINTIONS

Reinsurance is the acceptance by an insurer, known as a *reinsurer*, of all or part of the risk of loss of another insurer, called the *ceding company*. The original insurer is known variously as the ceding company, the reinsured, and the primary insurer. The successful negotiations between the insurer and reinsurer result in a reinsurance agreement. The agreement itself is referred to as a *treaty wording* or *excess contract*, depending upon the type of reinsurance coverage involved. The agreement provides for the primary insurer to reinsure a portion of a risk[1] by *ceding* a portion of its liability to the reinsurer; thus, *to cede* is to pass on to the reinsurer a portion of a risk. The act of reinsuring then is the acceptance by the reinsurer of such a cession of risk.

Retention, as used in reinsurance, may be defined as the amount of liability the ceding company retains for its own account. Retention may be expressed as a percentage or as a dollar amount. When expressed as a percentage of the total liability, the ceding company retains a certain percentage of the total liability insured under a policy. If it remains at risk for 30 percent of the policy limit, the ceding company passes the balance, 70 percent, on to the reinsurer. When the retention is expressed as a dollar amount, the primary insurer has at risk on any one policy up to the amount of the retention, the surplus liability being passed on to the reinsurer. If, for example, the retention for Company A were set at $5,000, the company would retain no more than that amount on any one risk, passing on any surplus liability to the reinsurer. On a $6,000 risk, the ceding company would retain $5,000 and pass $1,000 on to the reinsurer.

There are many more terms which have to be defined and examined. They will be discussed as they arise rather than be included here. The terms discussed above are sufficient for an understanding of the discussion of the functions of reinsurance to follow.

FUNCTIONS OF REINSURANCE

Reinsurance costs the primary insurer money, just as insurance costs the individual buyer of insurance money. Both have definite reasons for buying their particular product, and both strive to reduce

[1]*Risk* as used here has dual meanings. In pro-rata reinsurance, the risk reinsured is a portion of the specific liability assumed by the ceding company under a contract of insurance. In excess reinsurance, the risk reinsured is the excess portion of a loss.

their costs whenever it is practicable. Basically, the end to which an insurer buys reinsurance is to enable it to provide a better insurance market to its agents and to the public. A good insurance market has sufficient capacity to handle the bulk of risks offered to it during the normal course of its business day. It also is a stable market, both in terms of financial stability and market stability . . . it is not continually moving into and out of lines of insurance. A good insurance market is a competitive one, providing a good buy for the insurance buyer and thus a good market for its agents. The importance of reinsurance in providing ways for each insurer to be such a market varies by insurer. The success the insurer achieves in this effort is affected to a degree by how well it matches its reinsurance needs with reinsurance coverages. The reinsurance buyer should never lose sight of the particular reasons his company buys reinsurance, and if the basis for the reasons change, or cease to exist, the reinsurance coverage should be altered or removed altogether.

The reasons why insurers buy reinsurance are numerous. Reinsurance allows the insurer to increase its capacity to handle greater exposures. It assists the insurer in stabilizing his overall operating results from year to year. Reinsurance provides a medium for the spreading of risk throughout the insurance market. The effective working of the Law of Large Numbers is assisted by reinsurance through providing the insurer with a way to achieve size homogeneity in the risks it insures. Reinsurance provides a "banking facility" by easing the financial strain of rapid premium growth. It also provides an avenue whereby the insurer can quickly enter or withdraw from a geographical area. Finally, it often is the method used in mergers to handle the outstanding policies of the carrier being absorbed.

The primary function of reinsurance is to increase the insurer's capacity to accept larger exposures than it would otherwise be able to accept. This is accomplished in several ways. First, the ceding company may reinsure a portion of a particular risk on which the chance of loss is abnormally high. Through reinsurance, it can reduce its commitment, passing the excess exposure to the reinsurer. Secondly, the insurer can automatically increase its capacity by arranging with a reinsurer to automatically accept a portion of every risk it insures in a particular class of business, e.g., homeowners, commercial fire, etc. This answers the insurer's normal capacity requirement for everyday operations. It is able to accept larger lines on normal risks than its financial size would otherwise allow on a "gross" basis because the reinsurer assumes a portion of the liability, thereby leaving a "net" amount at risk in proper relation to the ceding company's financial size. Finally, the primary insurer's capacity to accept a concentration of risk in a geographical area is increased through reinsurance. Insurers used to maintain Sanborn Maps for every town in which they provided insurance coverage. The Sanborn Map showed, among other things, the location and construction of every building in the town. As a fire-daily was received by the underwriting department, the policy limits were written on the map. The underwriter could then determine his concentration of risk in the block and adjust his net line on the particular risk under consideration through reinsurance.

Today, Sanborn Maps are largely a thing of the past. Insurers depend upon competition from other insurers to limit their penetration in smaller communities and residential areas. However, many insurers still rely upon the maps to gauge their net lines on large office buildings in the hearts of our large cities.

Reinsurance can help the insurer by adding a degree of stability to the loss ratio. It provides a way for the insurer to stabilize its operations by spreading its heavy losses over a period of years through catastrophe reinsurance coverages. This stabilization effect does not guarantee the insurer a constant loss ratio. At best, reinsurance only removes the erratic motions the loss ratio might otherwise experience and puts in its stead a slow variation in loss experience.

Insurers may achieve a wide spread of risk through the long established practice of reciprocity. Reciprocity is the practice between primary insurers of placing reinsurance treaties on a reciprocal basis, one against another, so that the ceding company will only give a share of its treaty to a reinsurer who is able to offer another in return. Thus, each insurer involved in the transaction effectively increases the number of risks it insures by the number of risks its reciprocal partner insures. The object in participating in the insuring of as many different risks as possible is to allow the Law of Large Numbers to work as efficiently as possible for the insurer. This action reduces the overall effect on the insurer's loss ratio of a large total loss of a risk in the class. This practice effectively allows the insurer to substitute an infrequent 100 percent share of a large loss for more frequent, but much smaller shares (sometimes as little as 0.25 percent), of large losses. The higher frequency and smaller shares enables the insurer to more accurately predict, and thereby control, its loss ratio.

The underwriter's basic function is to increase his employer's chances of making a profit out of its insurance endeavor. He increases the "odds" of making a profit by two specific actions: establishing (1) quality homogeneity and (2) size homogeneity. First, he determines the quality of the risk to be insured and, if acceptable, places it in a rating category with risks with similar chances of loss. Through assigning different rates to risks presenting different chances of loss, the underwriter achieves quality homogeneity in each rating group. All risks with a $1.00 rate have a similar chance of loss. If the underwriter has been skillful in his quality grouping, each rating group will have a reasonable chance of realizing satisfactory loss experience.

The underwriter cannot rely upon quality grouping (quality homogeneity) alone and be confident of good loss experience year in and year out. He must achieve homogeneity in risk size as well. One way the underwriter can achieve size homogeneity is through reinsurance. The importance of grouping by size as well as by quality can be easily illustrated. Assume a perfect grouping of risks with a $1.00 rate per $100 of insurance and a probability of loss of 0.50 percent. Two hundred risks of $5,000 each would produce a premium of $10,000 (200 x 50 x $1.00). If the loss experience perfectly adhered to the loss probability, one half of one percent of the $5,000 risks, or one of the two hundred risks here, would be destroyed, yielding a loss ratio of exactly 50 percent ($5,000/$10,000). So far the grouping has both size and quality homogeneity. Now, what happens if a $30,000 risk is introduced into the group, and it is the one that is destroyed? A premium of $10,250 (199 x 50 x $1.00 plus 1 x 300 x $1.00) is produced, and the loss ratio becomes 292.7 percent.

The underwriter best fulfills his function when he achieves size as well as quality homogeneity in each rating class. Quality grouping is accomplished by basic risk selection and matching rate with probability of loss. Size grouping within each rating group is accomplished by a combination of having a sufficient spread to allow the efficient working of the Law of Large Numbers and reinsurance to limit the maximum size of risk insured. The importance of reinsurance in this area diminishes as the number of risks insured grows; however, as a practical matter, the need for reinsurance here seldom ceases to exist. To eliminate the use of reinsurance, the insurer must decline to accept limits of liability greater than those normal to a day's business activity. Such a rule, for example, would dictate that no policies covering single family residences may be issued in excess of $40,000. Enough dwellings exist up to this limit that the insurer is assured of getting a reasonable spread of risk in all groups within this class to enable the Law of Large Numbers to work in its favor, even on the $35,000 to $40,000 grouping. The same results could be obtained by ceding everything over $40,000 to the reinsurer. This would have the advantage of providing a better market for the agent because he would not have to issue two policies covering a dwelling whose amount at risk exceeded $40,000.

Another valuable function of reinsurance is the financing or "banking" facility reinsurance provides to the ceding company. The small, growing insurer often needs the financial assistance of the reinsurer. This need stems from the unearned premium reserve that state insurance regulations require insurers to maintain. Almost all of the expenses associated with placing business on the books are incurred and paid at the first of the policy period. Because state regulations require the entire premium paid by the insured be placed in an unearned premium reserve, the insurer has to draw funds from surplus with which to pay the initial expenses. With proportional reinsurance treaties, the reinsurer relieves the ceding company of the requirement of maintaining the unearned premium reserve on the portion of the risk reinsured. A commission is paid by the reinsurer to the ceding company for the premiums thus ceded. This "reinsurance commission" is similar to the commission the ceding company paid the agent for producing the business, except it is larger. The reinsurance commission covers the ceding company's expenses in acquiring and servicing the policies concerned. Through the assumption of a portion of the unearned premium reserve and the payment to the ceding company of a commission for the premiums ceded, the reinsurer has assisted the ceding company in financing its growth. The reinsurer has made immediately available to the ceding company cash with which to pay a portion of its expenses. This cash would have otherwise been tied up in an unearned premium reserve until it is fully earned.[2]

Another banking function reinsurance can provide is the reinsuring of a bulk of the premiums written in a class of business in order to improve the ceding company's ratio of surplus to unearned premium reserve. This ratio is used as a measure of the insurer's ability to pay claims in the event its premium income is exhausted. A high ratio indicates that the insurer has proportionally greater amount of surplus with which to pay losses than an insurer whose ratio is lower. On occasion, insurers, particularly young ones in growth situations, discover that this ratio is below the minimum requirements. Through reinsuring a large part of the premiums of a class or classes of business, the unearned premium reserve required to be maintained on the premiums ceded is passed on to the reinsurer. The commission dollars received are then applied to the surplus, thereby bringing the

[2]See page 43 for a discussion of unearned premium reserves and how they are earned.

ratio back to a more attractive level.

Under certain circumstances, insurer management may decide that the business being derived from a particular area is inherently unprofitable and beyond hope of improvement. Southern Florida provides a good example of an area where many carriers have ceased to provide property coverage because of windstorm losses. The same may be true of a line or class of business. In such circumstances, the decision may be made to get out of the area or class as quickly as possible. Along the same lines, management may decide to reduce the operating territory of the company to better utilize its present service facilities and agency force. In each of the above cases, the insurer is faced with a choice. It may either continue the policies issued in the area or class concerned until they expire or sell the entire amount at risk to another insurer. Quite often the latter choice is the action taken, with the "other insurer" being a reinsurer. The reinsurer in such cases seldom is a professional reinsurer; generally, it is a primary insurer actively writing in the area or class involved.

Reinsurance may be used as a vehicle to enter a new geographical area. The expansion of premium writings into a new area may be accomplished in two ways. First, a sales force may be established and a volume of business developed. Secondly, reinsurance contracts may be negotiated with a company in the area allowing the entering insurer to act as a reinsurer. The time required to build a sales force and develop a volume of business is often so long that the profits which originally attracted the insurer may have disappeared. Or, the insurer may find that it is unable to develop a profitable operation due to unfamiliarity with insurance practices in that area. This latter problem is encountered primarily when establishing a branch in a foreign country where both the language and practices are different. By acting as a reinsurer for a company in the area, the insurer is able to immediately enter the area and enjoy the profits on an established book of business. At the same time, the insurer can obtain a working knowledge of peculiarities in practices in the area so that if a direct entry is decided upon, it will be a well planned and executed one.

SOME BASIC RELATIONSHIPS

Throughout all transactions of reinsurance there are three basic relationships upon which the dealings are founded and the interpretation and equitable operation of the contracts rely. An understanding of these relationships is necessary for a sound understanding of the subject of reinsurance. First, the dealings must be in utmost good faith (*uberrimae fidei*). Secondly, the reinsurer must "follow-the-fortunes" of the ceding company. Finally, the reinsurer is not directly liable to the insured.

Utmost Good Faith

As in the normal law of contracts, the negotiations between the insurer and the reinsurer must be in utmost good faith (*uberrimae fidei*). This doctrine calls for full disclosure by the ceding company of every material fact which may relate to the risk to be reinsured. In treaty reinsurance, the contract covers an extended period of time and innumerable cessions. The rule of disclosure here applies to all cessions throughout the contract. The completion of negotiations and signing of the treaty wording is only the beginning.[3] Many risks to which the rule would apply if each were reinsured individually are to be reinsured under this one contract. Obviously, the ceding company is not required to fully disclose the many particulars surrounding each individual risk to be reinsured under the treaty; however, it is required to disclose the cession of specific risks which do not correspond to the exact type of risk contracted to be reinsured under the treaty. For example, accommodation risks which are accepted by the ceding company to accommodate an agent should be disclosed to the reinsurer. If it desires to pass such a risk to its treaty reinsurer, the ceding company should report the cession to the reinsurer. The report makes possible special handling by the reinsurer if such is required. A clause in the normal treaty wording provides for various "advices" by the ceding company. These advices lay the foundation for such continuing disclosure.

Follow-the-Fortunes

The follow-the-fortunes concept is designed to act as a guide on specific cases falling within the realm of the contract. If there is any doubt as to how a specific case is to be handled (this generally arises in a loss situation), the overriding rule is that the reinsurer should benefit in a manner similar to the ceding company. The reinsurer shares with the ceding company its proportion of the good "fortunes" of the business reinsured as well as the bad "fortunes." The purpose of this provision is to guide in the interpretation of the contract. When there is doubt, the parties are to interpret the contract so that the reinsurer shares its proportion of the burden with the ceding company.

[3]*Treaty Wording* may be defined as the signed agreement which constitutes the contract of treaty reinsurance between the ceding company and the reinsurer.

The follow-the-fortunes clause is designed to make the contract as flexible as possible and yet to ensure that the terms and intent of the contract are followed. This clause keeps the treaty wording as general as possible and yet makes provisions for the varied occurrences which may be expected during the course of normal operations.

The following are two follow-the-fortunes clauses in general use today.

I

The Ceding Company shall not be prejudiced by any inadvertent error, omission, or oversight to cede what may rightly fall under this agreement, or to do any of the acts or things provided by the terms of this contract. The intention of this agreement is that the Reinsurer shall follow the fortunes of the Ceding Company in all matters falling under this agreement.

II

The Reinsurer agrees to follow the fortunes of the Ceding Company in all respects as if being a party to the insurances.

Relationship of Reinsurer to Insured

Generally, the reinsurance agreement is a contract between the reinsurer and the ceding company. The reinsurer is not directly liable to the insured. In the event of failure on the part of the reinsurer, the ceding company is not relieved of having to pay the full amount of any claim arising out of a policy reinsured. The contract of insurance is between the insurer and the primary insurer. Failure of the reinsurer does not relieve the insurer's liability for payment of the portion of the liability reinsured.

The primary insurer, by virtue of its contract with the insured, has an insurable interest in the subject matter of the insurance. It is this insurable interest which the primary insurer is covering with the reinsurance. Thus, the contract is separate and distinct from that contract between it and the insured. This was nicely put in the decision in the case of *Stecket vs. Excess Insurance Company of America*, Ohio Supreme Court, November 22, 1939, 23 N.E. (2nd) 839, 136 Ohio St. 49: "Reinsurance is a contract whereby one for a consideration agrees to indemnify another wholly or partially against loss or liability by reason of a risk the latter assumed under a separate and distinct contract as insurer of a third party."

There are two exceptions to this rule. (1) The reinsurer is directly liable to the insured when there is a specific obligation arranged between the reinsurer and the insured. Such a case would be where the reinsurer's name actually appears on the policy of insurance; and (2) the reinsurer is also directly liable to the insured when it assumes the assets and liabilities of the ceding company with the intent of assuming direct liability to the insured. Such an outright purchase of the insurer by the reinsurer normally occurs when the insurer is in receivership.

ALTERNATIVES TO REINSURANCE

There are some alternatives to the use of reinsurance. In certain circumstances, these alternatives can satisfy some of the needs reinsurance otherwise fulfills. One such alternative is for the primary insurer to limit the amount of its possible loss by restricting the size of risk acceptance to minimal limits. There are two distinct disadvantages to this method. First, the insurer will have an agency problem. Its agents will experience difficulty in satisfying their clients' needs because the company will not take a line large enough to cover a client's entire exposure. The agent will have to place the remainder of the liability with another insurer, thereby causing much duplication of effort and at least doubling the amount of paperwork required. Secondly, the primary insurer will find that it has a smaller premium volume with which to meet expenses. If it were issuing policies for the full amounts required by the insured and reinsuring, the ceding company would have the reinsurance commission to apply to the cost of doing business. It will be issuing the same number of policies under both systems. The only difference between the two approaches is that by using reinsurance, the face of the policies will be for larger amounts. As a result, the premium volume is increased without increasing expenses other than acquisition expenses and premium taxes. It is evident that the desirable approach is for the primary insurer to utilize a form of reinsurance rather than severely restrict its underwriting limits.

Another possible alternative to reinsurance is the careful balancing of the various lines of insurance comprising the primary insurer's portfolio. This strategy is designed to permit the maximum compensating effect between the experience of each line. The purpose of such a plan is to even out the total portfolio experience to a reasonable variation from year to year. The insurer utilizing this method might try to maintain its rate of acceptances so the total premium volume in any one month is composed of 30 percent automobile premium, 20 percent property premium, 20 percent general liability premium, and 30 percent package premium. The formula would be carefully computed, based on the profitability of each class of business. The proper ratio is one which will result in the profits lost on the less profitable lines being more than compensated by the profits realized on the more lucrative lines.

Such a ratio is hard to establish and impossible at best to maintain. Furthermore, the balance does not definitely limit the primary insurer's commitment on any one risk nor does it protect it against heavy losses. The balancing of lines must be complimented by reinsurance to protect the primary insurer against the effects of catastrophes, to establish size homogeneity (if required), and to definitely limit its commitment on any one risk to proper proportions.

Coinsurance offers another alternative to the use of reinsurance. Coinsurance involves the joint issuance of a contract of insurance by two or more insurers. Each insurer is directly liable to the insured for a proportion of the losses incurred under the policy. This practice is normally insituted by a large general agent who automatically distributes the premium to the participating insurers. Commissions are increased because the companies pay the agent standard reinsurance commissions rather than general agency commissions. The practice of coinsurance does limit the commitment on any one risk to smaller proportions as does reinsurance. This practice, however, is discouraged by insurers because it removes selection of risk and rating control from the insurer to the agent. It has been found that the centralizing of acquisition and acceptance functions with the agent, who assumes no liability, often results in unsatisfactory underwriting experience.

A further practice which is often mentioned as an alternative to reinsurance, is the use of pools. The pooling of risks is not a true "alternative" for it is a specialized use of reinsurance. A pool may be defined as the association of a group of insurers for the specific purpose of the sharing of risk through reinsurance. It is made up of several to more than one hundred insurers who each reinsure part of the risks ceded to the pool. Risks of a specific class are automatically ceded to the pool, and the members then share in the premiums and claims in an established proportion.

The great value of a pooling arrangement is that each member's share of risks ceded to the pool can be smaller than it would be able to economically retain if it were passing unilaterally the excess above a low limit to a reinsurer. It is receiving in return small shares of many risks, thereby increasing its spread (by number of insureds) and maintaining its premium volume at a high level.

The use of pools can greatly increase the market's capacity. It can enable certain classes of risk to be written on a profitable basis which otherwise might be unprofitable. Pools are commonly used to meet the requirements of extra-hazardous classes of risk, such as the aviation hazard. Ellis Carson reflected on the value of pools when he wrote: "Another way in which American resources have been combined to meet demands for coverage in the domestic market for large and unique exposures has been through the formation of underwriting associations (pools) such as the F.I.A., The Associated Factory Mutual System, and more recently, the Nuclear Energy Insurance Association."[4]

The pool itself does not assume liability on risks ceded to it. It is simply a clearinghouse, or exchange, where the various premiums and losses ceded to the pool are divided among the individual pool members. It is a formal organization formed to facilitate the spread of risk between members.

CHAPTER SUMMARY

Reinsurance is a method whereby the insurer distributes its risks by giving off the whole liability, or some portion thereof, to another insurer with the object of reducing the amount of its possible loss. The original insurer is known as the ceding company or primary insurer, and the insurer accepting the reinsurance is known as the reinsurer. The ceding company cedes to the reinsurer liability in excess of the amount its financial structure can safely assume on any one risk. The reinsurer assumes liability for that portion of the risk ceded. The contract of reinsurance is between the primary insurer and the reinsurer, the insured having no recourse to the reinsurer. In the event of failure on the part of a reinsurer, the ceding company is not relieved of having to pay the full amount of the claim. Since the reinsurance contract is one of utmost good faith, negotiations leading up to the signing of the contract must include full disclosure of material facts. In the normal course of operations and in the event of dispute, the agreement is to be interpreted in such a manner that the reinsurer follows the fortunes of the ceding company as closely as possible.

Reinsurance is designed to satisfy many of the needs of the primary insurer. Some of the more important functions reinsurance performs are (1) to increase the ceding company's capacity, (2) to help stabilize the ceding company's operating results, (3) to attain a greater spread of risk through reciprocity, (4) to enable the ceding company to attain a degree of size homogeneity, (5) to furnish banking

[4]Ellis H. Carson, "The Domestic Reinsurance Market," *Best's Fire and Casualty News*, (March, 1962), pp. 20-25.

facilities to the primary insurer, (6) to enable the ceding company to withdraw from a class or line of business or geographical area within a short period of time, and (7) to enable an insurer to quickly enter a new area or class of business.

There are times when reinsurance does not serve the best interests of the primary insurer. Since reinsurance is a cost, the various alternatives to reinsurance should be utilized when they offer equal or better solutions to the problems at lower costs. Because of the many functions which reinsurance performs, the insurer will never be able to operate effectively without a certain amount of reinsurance coverage.

CHAPTER II

Facultative Reinsurance

REINSURANCE AGREEMENTS may be placed into three basic categories: facultative, automatic pro-rata, and excess reinsurance. Facultative reinsurance is the reinsuring of an individual risk with the reinsurer possessing the option to accept or reject the proposal. Automatic pro-rata reinsurance is an automatic reinsuring of many individual risks, the ceding company being bound to cede and the reinsurer being bound to accept the cessions. The reinsurer shares in the losses in the same proportion as it shares in the premium.[1] Excess reinsurance, as contrasted to automatic pro-rata, is the automatic protection against losses which exceed a pre-determined amount. The theoretical basis and functional characteristics of the facultative, automatic pro-rata, and excess forms of reinsurance are considered in this and the following chapters in order to furnish a theoretical background for the understanding of the operations of reinsurance.

FACULTATIVE REINSURANCE

The facultative method of reinsuring is the oldest form of reinsurance. Although largely replaced by the automatic pro-rata and excess forms, it still plays an important role in giving the insurer effec-

[1]Automatic pro-rata reinsurance agreements are often referred to as "Treaties". Strictly speaking, a "treaty" is a contract between the ceding company and the reinsurer setting forth the conditions for reinsuring a class or classes of business. Technically, any written agreement between the insurer and reinsurer providing for continuing cessions in one form or another is a treaty. Thus, we have facultative obligatory treaties, facultative excess treaties, surplus treaties, quota share treaties, etc. However, when the general term "treaty reinsurance" is used, the speaker is generally referring to the automatic pro-rata type of reinsurance (surplus and quota share). The unadorned term "treaty" when used throughout this book should be understood to be a general term encompassing automatic pro-rata reinsurance agreements only.

tive reinsurance coverage. Under facultative reinsurance, the ceding company is under no obligation to cede, and the reinsurer is under no obligation to accept a request for reinsurance on an individual risk. Both parties have the "facility" to act as they deem in their individual best interests without having to consider any prior contract. This form of reinsurance is often referred to as "street" reinsurance because the underwriter has to shop around for a reinsurer. He cannot rely upon the acceptance of a risk by any particular reinsurer.

The ceding company is essentially in the same relationship with the reinsurer as the insured is with the ceding company. The ceding company must furnish all of the details it has about the risk to be reinsured. If the reinsuring underwriter feels that there is not sufficient information to adequately underwrite the risk, he can, and often does, request additional information. If the reinsuring underwriter decides to accept the risk, he sets a rate which he feels adequate to cover the exposures involved.

Basic Characteristics of Facultative Reinsurance

The normal procedure which is followed in reinsuring a risk facultatively is for the ceding company to obtain reinsurance coverage before it issues the policy. This is done for two reasons: (1) to ensure that the rate which is to be charged by the reinsurer does not exceed the rate to be charged by the reinsured, and (2) to back up the underwriting judgment of the ceding underwriter. A primary underwriter often gains the benefit of the reinsurer's knowledge on a particular exposure through the means of a facultative cession.

A reinsurance policy (certificate) is issued by the reinsurer to the ceding company on every risk which is facultatively reinsured. The certificate indicates the amount of liability reinsured and the rate charged. It also contains various clauses indicating (1) that the reinsurance policy is to follow the original policy, (2) the renewal procedure, and (3) the claims procedure. The reinsurer is advised of any endorsements altering coverage; and the contract of reinsurance, under ordinary circumstances, follows the renewal of the original policy with no new reinsurance policy being required. The facultative reinsurance policy follows exactly the terms of the original policy and remains in force only so long as the original policy is in force.

Functions of Facultative Reinsurance

Originally, all reinsurance was transacted in the facultative form. Facultative reinsurance has been largely replaced by treaty reinsurance because of its high administrative costs. The facultative form will never become totally obsolete, however, because of its unique flexibility. It may be used in a variety of ways, such as in the reduction of commitment in a specific area. It may be used to reinsure any residual liability in excess of automatic reinsurance facilities, to reduce the ceding company's net retention on extra-hazardous risks as well as to restrict the amount of liability ceded to the treaty reinsurers, and to secure the reinsurer's underwriting experience on a particular hazard or exposure.

In the classes of business where the insurable interests are relatively stationary, for example standard fire insurance, the ceding company can become too heavily committed in a particular area. In order to reduce the exposure, the insurer may select various risks in the area concerned and reinsure them facultatively. As an alternative, it may reinsure the full liability on any new policy issued in this area. Often, the marine cargo underwriter will suddenly find that several ship-loads of cargo he has insured are being stored in the same warehouse awaiting delivery. When this happens, a facultative placement is hurriedly arranged so as to reduce his maximum possible loss in this warehouse to reasonable levels.

In the property lines, the automatic pro-rata treaty is the normal reinsurance vehicle. It is common practice for the primary insurer to have sufficient capacity in the treaty to absorb the bulk of the risks insured during the course of daily operations. There will be instances, however, when a risk will exceed the capacity of this treaty. Such excess liability is often facultatively reinsured so as to not increase the ceding company's maximum commitment on the risk above its original retention. Once the treaty capacity is exceeded, the surplus amount of liability reverts back to the ceding company for assumption or disposition elsewhere. Facultative reinsurance thus gives the ceding company the necessary tools for definitely limiting its commitment on any one risk to a reasonable sum. In the liability lines (including automobile) an excess contract is the common reinsurance vehicle. Its capacity is established to adequately absorb the normal limits insured; and facultative reinsurance is used to reinsure any liability in excess of the contract's capacity in a manner similar to the practice in the property lines.

Because of the nature of a particular risk, the ceding company may decide that its net retention under its automatic reinsurance facilities is too large. If the reinsurers will so allow, the ceding company may reduce its net retention by facultatively reducing its retention on a particular risk. A risk for which this procedure may be followed is one which, for some unique reason, is particularly hazardous. For example, the insurer's normal line on a frame, protected warehouse is

$100,000; and its surplus treaty has capacity to handle another $400,000. The ceding company receives a daily from an agent for the authorized maximum commitment on such a risk of $500,000; however, an inspection by company engineers reveals that it is within fifty feet of a large automobile paint shop. The exposure is such that the underwriter deems it prudent to reduce his retention under the treaty which presently stands at $100,000 retained liability and $400,000 reinsured. With the consent of the treaty reinsurers, the underwriter may reduce his retained liability to a more palitable sum, such as $40,000, by facultatively reinsuring $60,000 to another reinsurer.

Often, however, treaty reinsurers will not allow the ceding company to reduce its retention without proportionally reducing their commitmnet on the risk. Using the previous example, the reinsurer would probably want only $160,000; so the ceding company would have to facultatively reinsure the remaining $240,000.

Because of the desire for its treaty to be profitable and always in demand by reinsurers, ceding companies often facultatively reinsure any risk which has an abnormally high chance of loss instead of reinsuring it under the treaty. This practice is known as "underwriting" the treaty cessions, and it is an effective tool for improving or maintaining the experience under a treaty. It is particularly important if the treaty is used as the basis for reciprocity, for the better the profits are under the treaty, the easier it is to obtain and maintain reciprocal reinsurers.[2]

From time to time, the underwriter is presented with a proposal for insurance covering an unusual or extra-hazardous risk for which he is uncertain in his underwriting judgment. In such cases, it is not uncommon for him to place a portion of the liability facultatively, thus obtaining the reinsurer's underwriting assistance.

Facultative reinsurance is used to fulfill the more infrequent needs of the insurer. The bulk of these needs are to handle situations which represent a greater chance of loss than under normal circumstances. From the reinsurer's viewpoint, it can represent an easy way for its slim profits to completely disappear. However, by careful selection and rating and accepting only small shares of the liability offered, the facultative reinsurer is often able to make a profitable operation out of what could be considered the dumping grounds of the industry.

[2]See Chapter VII, The Art of Reciprocity, for a more detailed discussion of this subject.

Disadvantages of Facultative Reinsurance

As suggested in the preceding discussion, there are some serious disadvantages to the use of facultative reinsurance. These disadvantages have caused it to be largely replaced by the treaty form. They may be grouped into three general categories: (1) high cost of administration, (2) the general inefficiency of the system, and (3) high cost of coverage.

Because of the requirement of exchanges of a large quantity of information on each individual cession and of receiving an acceptance or refusal, the ceding company is almost limited to reinsuring with companies which are in the immediate vicinity. The clerical work involved in completing each cession, plus adding additional endorsements, premium notices, cancellation notices, and proofs of loss, can amount to many costly man hours during the life of the policy. The administrative costs alone could possibly exceed the overhead loading in the premium received from the insured, thereby cancelling any advantages gained by reinsuring.

The policy may not be issued to the insured until an affirmative answer is received from a reinsurer. The delay may cause a strain in relations between the prospect, the agent, and the insurer, with the fieldman being the unhappiest one of all.

Facultative reinsurance is high-cost coverage because there is not a guaranteed volume of business, and the business is normally of a volatile nature. These two factors jointly cause selection against the reinsurer. As a result, reinsurers usually give a smaller commission to the ceding company, thereby effectively raising the actual cost of the coverage to the ceding company.

Trends In Facultative Reinsurance

There has been a noticeable increase in the amount of facultative reinsurance placements in the past few years. This increase can be explained by several factors. The chief contributing factor being the growing practice of "underwriting" treaty cessions, i.e., the reduction of liability ceded under a treaty on an extra hazardous risk through facultative cessions, thereby improving the loss experience of the treaty reinsurers. Another factor is the ever-increasing value of inventories and equipment arising out of big business practices, thus creating the need for higher policy limits.

The evolution of the facultative method toward simplification of procedures has also contributed much to its increased usage. One of these is the development of the facultative excess concept. In the past, facultative placements were solely on a portion of the liability basis, i.e., the reinsurer would assume either a percentage of the policy limits or a stated dollar amount. It would share in every loss in relation to its participation to the total policy limits. Under a facultative excess agreement, the reinsurer only participates in losses which occur in excess of the ceding company's net retention. The economies of this form of facultative reinsurance result from the fact that the only handling required is to pay the reinsurance premium and collect for the few losses that exceed the retention, if any. The ceding company's net retention generally is sizeable, and the rate is correspondingly low. This lowers the insurer's reinsurance costs.

The facultative excess is generally used today on larger risks with a low chance of loss; e.g., a Class A multi-story office building. On such risks, the insurer can justify large retentions, thereby retaining the premium on what it hopes to be a profitable line. Regardless of these improvements, however, the fewer facultative placements an insurer has the lower will be the insurer's overall reinsurance costs.

CHAPTER SUMMARY

Facultative reinsurance is the form of reinsurance where the primary insurer is under no obligation to cede, and the reinsurer is under no obligation to accept a request for reinsurance on an individual risk. This is reinsurance of a single risk and is often called "street-type" reinsurance because the primary insurer has to go out in the street, so to speak, and try to obtain reinsurance coverage. There are three primary characteristics of this coverage: (1) The risk to be reinsured is underwritten by the reinsuring underwriter, who may accept it or reject it, and charge a rate which he feels is adequate for the risk assumed; (2) A separate reinsurance policy or "certificate" is issued covering each cession; and (3) The reinsurance policy follows the original policy, being automatically renewed if the original policy is renewed.

The functions of facultative reinsurance are (1) to reduce the ceding company's commitment in a specific area, (2) to handle surplus liability, (3) to reduce the share of liability ceded to the treaty reinsurers on specific risks, (4) to reduce the ceding company's net retained line on a specific risk, (5) to reinsure extra-hazardous or unusual risks which are not covered under automatic reinsurance arrangements, and (6) to enable the primary underwriter to obtain underwriting counsel from the reinsuring underwriter on a risk of questionable or of uncertain nature. The primary disadvantages in the use of facultative reinsurance are (1) its slowness and uncertainty, and (2) its high cost of administration.

CHAPTER III

Automatic Pro-Rata Reinsurance

AUTOMATIC PRO-RATA REINSURANCE is an obligatory reinsurance agreement whereby the ceding company is bound to cede, and the reinsurer is bound to accept the share of the risk to be reinsured as provided in the treaty. The reinsurer shares in the premiums and losses in the same proportion as it shares in the over all amounts at risk. The development of the treaty form of reinsurance marked a great step forward in the practice of reinsurance. Because of the new concept of obligatory cession and acceptance, a new area of reinsurance underwriting had to be developed. The result was "company underwriting," i.e., underwriting of the company management and underwriting policies rather than the underwriting of specific risks as is done with facultative reinsurance. Treaty reinsurance finds its greatest application in property coverages. Reinsurance of liability coverages is generally handled through the use of excess reinsurance (see Chapter IV). A plausable explanation of this is that treaty reinsurance is easily used by the property underwriter who is used to thinking in terms of "participating" in the coverage of a large or hazardous risk with other carriers. On the other hand, the liability underwriter generally thinks in terms of assuming the entire limit, or none at all, and therefore finds excess reinsurance of greater benefit and considerably less troublesome to handle.

The treaty is an obligatory contract in which both parties relinquish a portion of their freedom to act. Because the reinsurer relinquishes the right to underwrite the risks to be ceded, control is lost over the quality of business being assumed. The reinsurer must, therefore, receive a sufficient volume of business to result in a satisfactory average risk. Such an average risk would be (1) comparable to the average risk originally insured by the ceding company, and (2) yield a premium volume adequate to support the aggregate risk accepted. By requiring the treaty to meet these two requisites, the reinsurer will be reasonably assured of realizing a profit over the long run *if* the ceding company is underwriting on a profitable basis.

In order to yield a profit to the reinsurer, the ceding company is obligated to cede a certain portion of every risk that comes within the terms of the treaty. On the other hand, the ceding company is assured of a definite amount of reinsurance coverage on every risk accepted which falls within the scope of the treaty. The reinsurance coverage is guaranteed, no matter what the reinsurer might think of the individual risks ceded. Thus, it is obvious that under the treaty method of reinsuring, the individual risks ceded are only important insofar as their affect on the aggregate experience of all cessions. Therefore, the rate charged the primary insurer for the coverage, and the desirability of the treaty, is directly related to the over all experience of the treaty.

TYPES OF AUTOMATIC PRO-RATA REINSURANCE AGREEMENTS

There are several types of treaty reinsurance agreements all having predominately the same characteristics. The major variation between types are contained within the Operative Clause of the treaty wording. This clause outlines the scope of the treaty, indicating to which types of business the treaty will apply and in what manner. The procedure utilized in this section of the book is to examine the characteristics of the various types of treaties. Later, the characteristics common to all treaties are discussed in detail to complete the picture of automatic pro-rata reinsurance. It is hoped that a clearer understanding of what constitutes a treaty as opposed to the other forms of reinsurance will result by using this sequence of presentation.

The Surplus Treaty

The two types of treaties under which the vast bulk of automatic pro-rata reinsurance business is handled are the surplus treaty and the quota share treaty. The surplus treaty is the most widely used form of treaty reinsurance. The quota share treaty is generally reserved for places where the surplus form is not suitable. Of relatively minor importance are the varied "special" forms of treaties such as facultative obligatory, retrocession, and portfolio reinsurance which are used on infrequent occasions to meet special situations.

In this section, the surplus treaty is discussed through consideration of its identifying characteristics. It should be understood that these characteristics are in addition to the general treaty characteristics and functions discussed later in the chapter. In the following sections, the other types of treaties are considered in a similar manner in order to identify their individual characteristics and uses.

A surplus treaty is an automatic reinsurance agreement whereby the reinsurer is bound to accept, and the ceding company is bound to cede only the surplus liability in excess of a predetermined limit. The reinsurer contributes to the payment of losses in proportion to its share of the total limit of coverage. The ceding company's retention is that amount of liability which the ceding company must retain for its own account on any one risk before it may allot any liability to its surplus reinsurers. The capacity of a surplus treaty is normally explained in terms of the number of "lines" it contains. A line is equal to the ceding company's retention. For example, the ceding company's retention is $5,000; and it has a ten line surplus treaty. The capacity of the treaty to absorb liability in excess of the retention would be $50,000 (10 lines x $5,000).

A surplus treaty normally has several levels of retention, the size of the retention varying in direct proportion to the quality of the risk being reinsured. A class of risk of low quality representing a high chance of loss would have a lower retention than would a high quality class of risk representing a low chance of loss. The retentions vary by class according to chance of loss, not class of risk. Class A, the highest quality risk, will have a higher retention than Class D, the lowest quality risk. All risks insured must be fitted into a class and the retention applied as set out in the treaty wording. The amount of surplus liability in excess of the retention so established on each risk must be allotted to the surplus reinsurers.

Surplus Treaty Characteristics. The primary characteristic of the surplus treaty is that the percentage amount reinsured may vary from cession to cession. This is the result of the retention being set at a monetary level. There are two ways of stating the limits of a surplus treaty, those being (1) fixed line limit or limit per line as sum insured, and (2) variable line limit. There are two variable provisions, limit per line as maximum probable loss and variable lines per variable retention. The limit per line, or "line limit," is the maximum amount of liability which may be reinsured per line. In the past, the majority of reinsurers accepted liability under a treaty in relation to a line, i.e., they accepted a line (or one-half of a line) or some fraction thereof when underwriting the treaty. If a reinsurer assumed liability for one-half of a line, his maximum liability was one-half of the ceding company's retention. The line limit was a practical expression of the limit of liability per reinsurer. The underwriting rule of thumb is that a reinsurer should not accept a greater liability under a treaty than the retention of the ceding company. Even though the practice today is for the reinsurer to express its share of a treaty as a percentage of the entire capacity of the treaty, the line limit is still a valid limitation on the ceding company.

If the limit per line is in relation to the sum insured, the maximum amount that can be ceded to the surplus reinsurers is definitely fixed. The sum insured is the face amount of the policy. A ten line surplus treaty with a capacity of $50,000 (a line is $5,000), can absorb liability up to $50,000 on a single risk if the limits per line are in relation to the sum insured. The maximum amount the ceding company can retain is $5,000, no matter how good the risk.

If, on the other hand, the treaty provides for variable line limits, the treaty's capacity is not so restricted. Assuming the Probable Maximum Loss (PML) estimate on a $200,000 risk is 10 percent, or $20,000, the ceding company's retention would be $20,000 (one line is equal to the estimate of probable maximum loss), thereby increasing the capacity of the same ten line treaty to $200,000 (as opposed to $50,000 as above). This would be an example of a treaty with the capacity varying according to the limit per line as probable maximum loss. Under the probable maximum loss basis, the ceding company's retention is expressed as the probable maximum loss on any particular risk reinsured instead of a schedule of retentions in dollar terms. All of the lines in a treaty using this basis will be equal to PML. In operation, the ceding company's underwriters estimate the probable maximum loss on a particular risk, and the retention is set at that level. The obvious advantage of this system is that this gives the ceding company flexibility in the amount its surplus treaty can absorb. The other variable line limit provision in use today provides for the *number* of lines in the treaty to vary with the ceding company's retention. If the company retains less than a specified amount net, only one line may be ceded to the treaty. On the other hand, as the retention goes up, so does the number of lines available under the treaty. This clause gives the ceding company a great deal of capacity to write risks of excellent construction, protection, and favorable occupancy, and yet it protects the reinsurers from receiving heavy cessions on low quality, less desirable risks.

The disadvantages of the fixed line limit basis are two-fold. First, the ceding company's treaty capacity is strictly limited. Secondly, the premiums ceded to each reinsurer may be so small on the good risks that the administration will cost more than the premiums can absorb. This would be especially true on the good risks with low estimates of probable maximum loss and low rates.

The disadvantage of the variable line limit, particularly the limit per line as the probable maximum loss, is that too frequently the probable maximum loss estimate turns out to be only a small fraction of the actual loss experienced. Engineers and underwriters are too optimistic in their estimates. A good example of this is seen in the antics of Hurricane Frieda of 1962, when she played havoc with a transmission line risk in Oregon. The loss amounted to approximately 50 percent, whereas the PML had been estimated at around 2 percent. Because of the inaccuracy of the PML estimates, reinsurers tend to shy away from treaties whose limits are stated in terms of PML. Only if the ceding company is of the highest quality and reflects solid conservatism in its underwriting policy will a reinsurer accept such a treaty. Even when such a treaty is established, the ceding company is not given complete freedom. A maximum limit is always included in the contract and may be expressed as a dollar amount ("but in no case more than $25,000") or as a limiting PML ("no less than a PML of 15 percent").

In order to minimize the disadvantages of the fixed limit, the ceding company sets the capacity of its surplus treaty so that the treaty can absorb the vast bulk of risks insured during normal operations. A second surplus can be placed on top of the first surplus to absorb the larger risks which exceed the capacity of the underlying or first surplus.

The second characteristic of the surplus treaty is that it can be built into layers. A primary insurer may have a first surplus treaty, a second surplus treaty, and even a third surplus treaty. Normally, there will be different reinsurers participating in each treaty. The various treaties operate exactly in the same fashion as the first surplus except that the underlying surplus enjoys priority over the ones above it. The capacity of each underlying surplus must be exceeded on an individual risk before the next surplus can become interested. For example, Company A has a 1st, 2nd, and a 3rd surplus treaty. Each treaty has a capacity of $50,000. A risk with surplus liability in excess of the retention of $70,000 would be allotted to the surplus reinsurers as follows: 1st Surplus = $50,000, 2nd Surplus = $20,000, 3rd Surplus = $0. A $130,000 surplus risk would be allotted in a similar manner: 1st Surplus = $50,000, 2nd Surplus = $50,000, 3rd Surplus = $30,000.

Operation of the Surplus Treaty. In order to complete the description of the surplus treaty, a consideration of how it functions from cession to cession is necessary. As discussed earlier, the surplus treaty is a proportional, or pro-rata, agreement. Despite the fact that there are retentions in the surplus treaty, it remains a pro-rata agreement.

To recall the earlier discussion, a pro-rata reinsurance agreement is one in which the ceding company and reinsurer share, in a fixed proportion, the premiums, liability, and claims. Although the surplus treaty appears to be in conflict with this definition, it is not, because of one factor: the fixed proportion. The surplus treaty proportion varies with each individual risk reinsured. Once the amount of liability to be ceded on a particular risk has been determined, the proportional sharing becomes fixed on that risk. The reinsurer then shares the same proportion of all claims and premiums applicable to that particular risk as its reinsured liability bears to the total amount of reinsurance.

For example, Company A reinsures a $10,000 risk under its first surplus treaty, the premium on which is $100. The retention is set at $5,000. The liability ceded to the reinsurer is equal to the liability which exceeds the retention. The amount of liability ceded is $5,000, and the reinsurer receives $50 for assuming the liability. The ceding company retained 50 percent of the liability, ceding 50 percent to the reinsurer. For the coverage, the ceding company shared with the reinsurer 50 percent of the premiums. If this risk were to result in a $500 claim, the ceding company would be responsible for 50 percent and the reinsurer for 50 percent, or $250 each. The retention under a surplus treaty does not have to be exceeded by a loss before the reinsurer becomes interested. Under this form of reinsurance, the reinsurer shares a definite proportion of all claims, no matter how small.

Another way to look at the proportional concept is by considering the liability shared. In the earlier example, the ceding company is responsible for half the risk and the reinsurer responsible for the other half. One third of the property is destroyed. Whose third has been destroyed, the ceding company's or the reinsurer's? Obviously, it would be absurd to try to set out which part of the risk is the ceding company's and which is the reinsurer's. Thus, the parties agree in advance that any losses will be shared in the same proportion as the total liability under the policy.

The method of allotting liability to the various reinsurers participating in the treaty should also be considered. Fundamentally, all reinsurers in the same surplus treaty share the liability ceded on an equal basis according to their share of the treaty. There is no priority among reinsurers of the same treaty; however, there is priority between reinsurers of different surplus treaties. For example, if there were ten reinsurers in Company A's ten line first surplus treaty, and

Company A's retention is $5,000, the capacity of the treaty is $50,000. The liability on a risk insured for $55,000 would be allotted as follows: Company A, $5,000, and each reinsurer, $5,000. The liability on a risk insured for $25,000 would be allotted in this manner: Company A, $5,000; each reinsurer, $2,000 ($20,000 being ceded to the treaty, each reinsurer receiving ten percent of the ceded liability).

In the above example, the second surplus reinsurers were not allotted a share of the liability because the capacity of the first surplus, which enjoys priority, had not been exceeded. Whenever the capacity of the first surplus is exceeded, the surplus amount is allotted to the second surplus reinsurers in a manner similar to the way it is allotted to the first surplus reinsurers.

There is an exception to the mandatory requirement that the ceding company allot all surplus liability in excess of its retention to its first surplus reinsurers. It may cede the entire liability, or a portion thereof, on a risk outside the treaty if such action appears to be in the best interests of the reinsurer. The provision is designed to give the ceding company the ability to "underwrite" the treaty. In this way, it is able to improve the experience of the treaty through reinsuring outside the treaty risks of a doubtful nature which might adversely affect the treaty experience. Unfortunately, in certain cases, uninformed ceding companies utilize this clause to pass on to a pet reinsurer the very cream of the risks written, thus worsening the experience of the treaty rather than improving it. Such a company soon finds its "stable" reinsurance market is a thing of the past. No reinsurer is willing to accept a share of such a company's treaty except at a drastically reduced commission.

Functions of the Surplus Treaty. The surplus treaty has one basic function in addition to the general functions of treaty reinsurance. It gives the primary insurer an efficient way to establish size homogeneity. The surplus treaty places within the ceding company's grasp the ability to control the size of its retained liability in order to allow the Law of Large Numbers to operate with maximum efficiency. The smaller the variance by size from the average risk insured per class, the greater will be the predictability of experience of that class. The surplus treaty imparts an element of size homogeneity to the primary insurer through the working of the retention. The retention effectively cuts off all variance above a certain level of liability in each class, thereby definitely limiting the variance to a small margin. The reinsurers absorb the wide variances in size.

Disadvantages of the Surplus Treaty. There are two primary disadvantages in the use of surplus treaty reinsurance, one from the aspect of the ceding company and the other from the reinsurer's viewpoint. The disadvantage to the ceding company is the relatively high cost of administration associated with this type of treaty. The expense of having an underwriter determine the retention on each individual risk to be reinsured, coding and reporting to reinsurers, and of allotting the premiums and claims in the proper proportions to each reinsurer, is an expensive process. The cost is considerably less, however, than the costs of doing the same thing with facultative reinsurance.

The disadvantage to the insurer presented by the surplus treaty is its inherent characteristic of selection against the reinsurer. Selection comes about when the ceding company, by virtue of having a higher retention on good quality risks than on poor ones, retains a larger portion of the good risks and a smaller portion of the bad risks. In this way, the ceding company capitalizes on the profits of the good business and reduces its losses on the poor business. The reinsurer will be getting a large share of the poor business while getting only a small share of the good business. As a result of manipulating the retention, the ceding company may realize a higher rate of profit on the same business than the reinsurer. The reinsurer reduces the disparity by ensuring that the retentions are set so as to allow it to receive an equitable share of the good risks as well as its share of the poor ones. The careful negotiation of the retention schedule still will not yield the reinsurer the same profits as the ceding company. As a consequence, the reinsurer seeks to protect itself further by requiring that no cessions may be made outside the treaty unless it is in the interests of the reinsurers. The reinsurer accomplishes two things through this provision. First, the only cessions outside the treaty are those which will improve the treaty's profitability. Secondly, there will be a sufficient volume of risks ceded to the treaty to allow the reinsurer to realize a spread of liability in order to give it the benefit of the Law of Large Numbers.

The Quota Share Treaty

The quota share treaty is an automatic reinsurance agreement whereby the ceding company is bound to cede, and the reinsurer is bound to accept a fixed percentage of every risk written by the ceding company on an agreed class of business. The operative clause sets out the percentage of the risks to be reinsured. This clause also includes a definite dollar limit or maximum over which the reinsurer is not willing to be committed on any one risk, e.g., "five percent of every risk insured, not to exceed $10,000 on any one risk." As further protection, it is customary for the agreement to state that an agreed percentage must be retained by the ceding company. This ensures that the ceding company is not able to write poor business and escape any losses through reinsuring facultatively its share of the risk.

Quota Share Treaty Characteristics. The most outstanding characteristic of the quota share treaty is that within the same line of business, it is considerably more profitable to the reinsurer than the surplus treaty. Because the reinsurer is sharing each risk on the same basis as the ceding company, there is the conspicuous absence of selection against the reinsurer which is inherent in the surplus type. The quota share treaty, however, passes on a large share of the profits that would otherwise be retained by the ceding company. Because of the profitability of the quota share treaty, it is in wide demand by reinsurers; consequently, the primary insurer normally can get a better reinsurance commission than with a surplus treaty. The ceding company is able to reduce its commitment on each risk to small pieces, but it does not give any degree of size homogeneity to the ceding company as does the surplus treaty.

Functions of the Quota Share Treaty. Because of the cost of the quota share treaty in terms of profits passed on to the reinsurer, it is best suited to perform rather specialized functions which are of a relatively short term nature. The quota share treaty furnishes a greater capacity for a small primary insurer with limited surplus. The smaller company is normally required to utilize a quota share treaty until it has built up a book of business of reasonable size; then, reinsurers will normally allow it to change to a surplus treaty.

The quota share treaty is normally used by a ceding company when it is entering a new area or new class of business. The reason behind its use here is exactly the same as for the previous function, i.e., to entice the reinsurers to accept a share of a treaty covering unknown experience with a restricted spread. An insurer desiring to participate in the profits being realized in an area in which it does not write directly, may do so by acting as a quota share reinsurer for an insurer writing in the area concerned. This allows the "reinsurer" to participate directly in the profitable business without having to expend great capital sums in establishing a sales force and service facilities in the area. The quota share treaty is also used by groups of companies in order to give the maximum support possible to one or more of the weaker companies in the group. Support by the larger and financially stronger members is accomplished by having the weaker members act as quota share reinsurers for a portion of the larger carrier's most profitable line of business. This effectively passes a substantial amount of profits on to the weak members, thereby building up their surplus without direct financial support from the controlling company.

Facultative Obligatory Treaty

The facultative obligatory treaty, or reinsurance open cover as it is often called, is an automatic reinsurance agreement whereby the ceding company is at its option to cede, and the reinsurer is bound to accept a share of certain defined risks underwritten by the ceding company. Since this is partly facultative and partly treaty reinsurance, there is some disagreement as to whether it is treaty or facultative reinsurance. It is included here under the treaty category because it has the more important characteristics of the treaty and lacks the most important characteristic of the facultative. The reinsurer lacks the option to reject; it no longer has the "facility" to underwrite the cession and to reject it. It has all of the major characteristics of the treaty and could well be considered a surplus or quota share treaty with the clause allowing cessions outside the treaty broadened to allow such cessions whenever the ceding company desires to do so. In fact, it has been referred to as the equivalent of a second or third surplus treaty.

The primary functions of the facultative obligatory treaty is to stand on top of a surplus treaty in order to give the ceding company automatic reinsurance in excess of the capacity of its surplus treaty. If it were not for the existence of this open cover, the ceding company would have to utilize the expensive facultative method for placing the excess liability every time the capacity of its surplus treaty is exceeded. A further valuable use of the facultative obligatory treaty is that of giving the primary insurer automatic reinsurance arrangements to handle risks of a special nature of irregular occurrence. For example, in certain areas during the harvesting season, an accumulation occurs of insured cotton in warehouses and at queyside. The facultative obligatory treaty gives the ceding company a way to automatically reduce its commitment in any area where an accumulation of cotton occurs.

This is not the most desirable form of reinsurance coverage for the reinsurer. The treaty does not guarantee an even flow of business, nor can it be expected to give an average spread of risk. As a consequence, the reinsurer cannot expect to realize any stability of experience and must be prepared for wide fluctuations in experience from year to year. Because of the great danger that the ceding company will place into this treaty primarily extra hazardous risks, reinsurers are cautious as to whom they cover with such an agreement. If, however, the primary insurer represents a good moral hazard, the reinsurer is fairly happy to grant such a cover as the treaty presents the likelihood of obtaining a better spread of the ceding company's facultative portfolio than the reinsurer would get if it were to remain on a casual facultative basis. Further, as the ceding company's premium volume grows, the reinsurer might be able to convert the facultative obligatory treaty into a second or third surplus treaty.

Special Forms of Treaty Reinsurance

Besides the basic treaties discussed above, there are a few notable "special types" of treaty reinsurance which have a more specialized use, but which are used often enough to merit a short investigation here. The types to be considered in this section are the retrocession treaty and portfolio reinsurance.

The Retrocession Treaty. A retrocession is the term used to describe the reinsuring of liability assumed through reinsurance. Just as the primary insurer seeks to limit its possible loss, so does the reinsurer strive to limit its losses through retroceding a portion of its liability. The reinsurers who accept a retrocession of liability are known as retrocessionaries. In such a transaction, the reinsurer who is ceding liability is known as the retrocedent.

The retrocession agreement may be any one of the various forms of reinsurance, i.e., facultative, automatic pro-rata, or excess. There is no difference in principle between reinsurance and retrocession. In a retrocession, the reinsurer is only retroceding a share of the liability received through reinsurance. The reason for such a policy is to allow the reinsurer to reduce the probable accumulation which occurs through having treaties with several ceding companies whose direct business is derived from the same geographical area.

The quota share agreement is the most common type of retrocession contract. Surplus agreements are less common due to the difficulty of establishing retentions on risks to be retroceded as well as the "selection" characteristic of the surplus discussed earlier. In order to do set retentions, the retrocedent would have to require a relatively comprehensive set of bordereaux from its ceding companies, a requirement which is fast becoming a thing of the past. Therefore, the reinsurer is inclined to pass over the surplus treaty in favor of the quota share which does not require all of the careful work and costly administration.

The selection against the retrocessionaire in the surplus treaty is compounded when the reinsurer places a surplus retrocession treaty on top of its surplus treaties. In order to avoid such a situation, the retrocessionaires discourage the use of the surplus in favor of the quota share, which passes on to them the profits exactly as received by the retrocedent. An excess of loss retrocession agreement is used for the same reason and in the same manner as the excess of loss reinsurance agreement. It is normally used to protect the reinsurer from a heavy loss under assumed excess of loss liability, the rate being expressed as a percentage of the excess reinsurance premium received by the retrocedent.

In order to retain as much of its small profit as possible, reinsurers utilize the practice of reciprocity to a great extent, far greater in fact, than the same practice is used among primary insurers in this country. By utilizing reciprocity in retrocessions, reinsurers can maintain their premium volume and their profits and yet enjoy the benefits of retrocession coverage.

Portfolio Reinsurance. Portfolio reinsurance is the reinsuring of 100 percent of a block of direct business, or a portion thereof, by the primary insurer. Portfolio reinsurance has three basic areas of use: (1) to transfer bulk, unearned liability in a treaty in the transfer of automatic pro-rata reinsurers, (2) in geographical underwriting, and (3) in assisting in financial management. A portfolio of unearned premiums may be transferred from the retiring treaty reinsurer to the assuming reinsurer. This borders on not being truly classified as portfolio reinsurance, *per se*, because one of the implied characteristics of portfolio reinsurance is that it is a single transaction. Portfolio reinsurance does not provide for the continued cession of liability but rather for a single bulk cession of liability resulting from the acceptance of many individual insurances on the part of the ceding company.

The need for portfolio reinsurance may arise out of the desire by the ceding company to completely retire from a geographical area or line of business as quickly as possible. It accomplishes this by totally reinsuring its liability in that area to a reinsurer, the transaction being portfolio reinsurance. The primary insurer may also utilize portfolio reinsurance when its ratio of surplus to unearned premium reserve has fallen below the required minimum as established by the state regulatory bodies. In such circumstances, the primary insurer solves this problem by reinsuring a sufficient percentage of its book of business to bring the ratio back to the required level. Such an act of reinsuring constitutes portfolio reinsuring and is the third usage of portfolio reinsurance.

CHARACTERISTICS OF AUTOMATIC PRO-RATA REINSURANCE

Automatic pro-rata, or "treaty" reinsurance as it is commonly called, was a major development in reinsurance coverage. The advantages of speed, automatic coverage, and lower administrative costs over facultative reinsurance were necessary in order to allow primary insurers to transact insurance coverage on the scale our market demands today. It is not the entire answer, as excess reinsurance, when used properly, offers some advantages over the treaty form and will be considered later. The previous discussion of the types of treaties identified them by the peculiar characteristics which enable them to perform specific functions in addition to the general functions of treaty reinsurance. The following discussion presents the common characteristics of all pro-rata agreements which imparts to them their common functions. The knowledge required for setting up a reinsurance program demands a thorough understanding of these characteristics and how they are developed. These characteristics as discussed here are a result of the various clauses comprising the contract, an example of which is included in Appendix A.

The Liability of the Reinsurer and the Ceding Company

Under the treaty, the liability of the reinsurer commences simultaneously with that of the ceding company. If the risk insured falls within the scope of the treaty, the moment the ceding company is bound the reinsurer is bound for its proportion of the liability. If a loss were to be incurred by the insured immediately after the effective date of the policy and before the ceding company can make the entry on the "daily" showing the cession of the liability, the reinsurer will still be liable for its proportion of the loss. The rule in cases of this nature is that if the normal underwriting procedures would have required a cession of liability, the reinsurer is liable for that proportion of the loss, even if for some reason it was not informed of the cession. An "errors and omissions" clause is a relatively standard clause included in the treaty wording which covers such instances. The clause might read like this: "The ceding company shall not be prejudiced by any inadvertent error, omission or oversight to cede what may rightly fall under this agreement, provided that any such mistake or omission shall be corrected as soon as discovered."

Reinsurance Premium

The premium paid by the ceding company to the treaty reinsurer is a percentage of the original premium paid by the insured. The reinsurance premium is determined by the percentage of the total liability passed on to the reinsurer and is equal to the corresponding percentage of the total premium paid to the ceding company by the insured. For example, John Simon pays $100 to Company A for $10,000 coverage against loss by fire. If Company A passes 50 percent of the liability, $5,000, on to its treaty reinsurer, the amount of premium paid by Company A for this coverage would be 50 percent of the premium paid by John Simon, or $50. The premium paid to the treaty reinsurer is thus adequate only so long as the ceding company's underwriting is accurate, and the premium charged the insured is adequate. In the classes of business where the rates are closely regulated by the state, the rates so established are often inadequate. In such instances, the premium received by the treaty reinsurer is also inadequate.

Reinsurance Commission

A commission is given to the ceding company by the treaty reinsurer. The reinsurance commission is designed to compensate the ceding company for acquisition costs, costs of keeping the business on the books, the costs of administering the treaty, and taxes associated with the business reinsured. This is the basic commission given by the reinsurer, and, in the United States, it may range anywhere from a low of 28 percent to a high of 47 percent.

The level of the basic commission is determined basically by two factors: the expense ratio of the ceding company and the profitability of the treaty. Assume for the moment that the ceding company's loss ratio is 57 percent, and its expense ratio is 36 percent, yielding a combined ratio of 93 percent. It would seek a minimum of 36 percent commission from its reinsurers in order to cover its expenses on the transaction. Because of the satisfactory loss ratio, the ceding company might be able to negotiate a higher commission of 37 or 38 percent. It would then be in the position of realizing a "guaranteed" profit of one or two points, as the commission it receives is higher than its expenses by that amount. Such circumstances are rare because reinsurers try to avoid guaranteed profit situations. Ceding companies have been known to cede a great volume of poor business and make a profit at the reinsurer's expense before the treaty could be cancelled. The normal arrangement is some form of contingent commission in addition to the basic commission. This will yield the ceding company essentially the same profit and also ensure that the ceding company will maintain good underwriting practices.

Another commission often paid by the reinsurer for treaty reinsurance is an "over-riding" commission. This is normally a relatively small commission, approximately 1 or 2 percent. The over-riding commission is designed to meet one of two situations. Some reinsurers do not include in the calculation of the basic commission the cost of administering the treaty on the part of the ceding company. Since this is another cost incurred in excess of that associated solely with the direct business, an overriding commission designed to cover this cost is justified *if* it is not considered in the basic commission. The other instance such a commission is used is in situations where the reinsurer is receiving unilaterally a share of a treaty for which the ceding company normally requires reciprocity. A professional reinsurer, a reinsurer whose business is solely that of accepting reinsurance, is unable to reciprocate. In order to induce the primary insurer to let it participate in the treaty, the reinsurer may give the primary insurer an over-riding commission to replace, to a degree, the profit it would otherwise receive by reciprocally reinsuring.[1]

It is a normal policy for a reinsurer to give a profit, or contingent commission, if the ceding company so desires. The profit commission is designed to return to the ceding company a portion of the profits passed on to the reinsurer under the treaty. The profit commission may either be a flat percentage of the profits, or it may be included in a "sliding-scale" commission. The flat percentage commission may be based either upon a three years' average of profits or on a loss carry forward basis. On a loss carry forward basis, all losses are carried forward from year to year until they are exceeded by profits before any profit commission is paid. The commission paid normally ranges from a low of 10 percent to a high of 20 percent of the profit realized. This may be either a flat rate determined by the bargaining position of the ceding company, or it may be a sliding-scale, yielding a profit commission which varies with the average profit.

The sliding scale basic commission encompasses both the flat basic commission plus the profit commission. The level of commission paid varies with the loss experienced for the particular year in consideration. Normally, there is no three years' average or carrying forward of losses under this system. A minimum and maximum commission is payable, no matter how good or how bad the experience. The minimum commission is normally lower than a basic commission given under the other methods. For example, the minimum commission on a sliding scale basis may be 32 percent, whereas the same company might rightfully expect a 35 percent basic commission under the other methods. As the loss ratio experienced under the

[1]See the section on Professional Reinsurer vs. Reciprocity in Chapter VI for a detailed discussion of this area.

treaty falls, the commission paid increases up to the maximum commission allowed. The following is an example of a clause setting forth a sliding scale commission.

> The Reinsurer will allow to the Company a provisional commission of 32½% (thirty-two and one half percent) calculated on the net reinsurance premiums received by the Reinsurer under this agreement. As of the 31st day of December in any year during which the agreement is in force the provisional rate of commission shall be adjusted in accordance with the following scale:

IF LOSS RATIO IS	RATE OF COMMISSION
Less than 46%	42 %
46 but less than 47%	42½%
47 but less than 48%	41½%
48 but less than 49%	41 %
49 but less than 50%	40½%
50 but less than 51%	40 %
51 but less than 52%	39½%
52 but less than 53%	39 %
53 but less than 54%	38½%
54 but less than 55%	38 %
55 but less than 56%	37½%
56 but less than 57%	37 %
57 but less than 58%	36½%
58 but less than 59%	36 %
59 but less than 60%	35½%
60 but less than 61%	35 %
61 but less than 62%	34½%
62 but less than 63%	34 %
63 but less than 64%	33½%
64 but less than 65%	33 %
If loss ratio is 65% or over	32½%

> The "loss ratio" shall be arrived at by dividing — (a) The net reinsurance premiums for the period to the 31st day of December plus the unearned premium reserve for the period less the unearned premium brought forward from the preceding period into (b) The claims paid for the period to the 31st day of December plus the reserve for outstanding claims at that date less the outstanding reserve for the preceding period.

The sliding scale type of commission tends to level out the experience under the treaty, the reinsurer returning a larger portion of the profits in good years and a smaller portion in poorer ones. One factor should be considered: no matter how profitable the treaty is, after the loss ratio drops below 46 percent, as in the case above, the ceding company no longer shares in the additional profits. On the reinsurer's end, the commission given cannot drop below 32½ percent, no matter how high the loss ratio.

Criterion for Risk Assignment

The vast majority of treaties being negotiated are to cover an insurer who is actively writing business. This, of course, means that at any given moment the company will have a certain number of policies about to expire, some mid-way in the policy period, and still others just issued or in the process of being issued. When such a situation exists, one of the clauses in the treaty has to set out just which risks will be ceded under the treaty. For example, Company A has its treaty with Reinsurer R. As of December 31, at 12:00 P.M. the treaty is cancelled and placed with Reinsurer S. A loss occurs January 10, on a policy which became effective December 25. Which reinsurer is liable for this loss? There are basically two methods of solving this situation: (1) the premiums earned basis, and (2) the policies attaching basis. These provisions are designed to set out clearly which liability is ceded to which reinsurer.

The premiums earned basis assigns liability to the reinsurer who is actively reinsuring the ceding company as the premium is being earned on each individual policy. The reinsurer is only reinsuring the ceding company for the amounts at risk during the treaty year. It is not responsible for losses occurring either before or after the treaty year. A treaty year is the yearly period commencing when the treaty becomes effective, expring exactly one year later. The purpose of the treaty year is to break up the life of a treaty into units for accounting purposes. Items which are based upon the treaty year standard are the loss ratio, the profit commission, unearned premium reserve, and outstanding claims reserve.

Under the premiums earned basis, if the treaty year commences at 12:01 A.M. on January 1, and ends at 12:01 P.M. on December 31, the reinsurer will receive the premiums applicable to the liability covered during this period, i.e., the earned premium. It would likewise be liable for any losses occurring between these two dates.

The earned premium basis for risk assignment is simply the standard earned premium concept upon which the unearned premium reserves are established in the United States for regulatory purposes. Briefly, the earned premium concept may be explained thusly: an annual premium paid by the insured is "earned" at the rate of 1/12 per month, the entire premium being earned at the end of the twelfth month (expiry). On a three year policy, the premium would be earned at the rate of 1/3rd per year, or 1/36th per month, and completely earned at the end of the three years when the policy expires. As far as the treaty reinsurer is concerned, under the normal annual policy, it will receive the premiums earned for the periods of the policy life during which the treaty is in force. If an annual policy were one half earned at the beginning of the treaty year and expires six months later, the reinsurer will receive its share of one half of the annual premium or six months of earned premium at the rate of 1/12th per month.

In operating under the earned premium basis, the incoming reinsurer assumes the unearned premium reserve from the outgoing reinsurer. The outgoing reinsurer is then released from all liability under the treaty – there is no run-off of liability. The unearned premium reserve so transferred is called a "portfolio," the new reinsurer being said to have "assumed the incoming portfolio." Upon termination of the treaty, the reinsurer returns to the ceding company the "portfolio" of unearned premium reserves. The ceding company then passes it to the new reinsurer who assumes the liability for all losses under the treaty which occur after the effective date of the treaty.

There are three basic advantages of the earned premium method. There is no long run-off of liability – the reinsurer breaks away from the treaty upon expiry. Only a reserve for outstanding claims has to be maintained for the losses which occurred during the time the outgoing reinsurer was at risk. Finally, the reinsurer can cancel, if the experience is bad, and immediately cut off further losses. The disadvantages of the system are that the incoming reinsurer is liable for the previous years' underwriting over which it has no control. If there is a bad year, the reinsurer can cancel, leaving the ceding company out on the limb with a poor portfolio to place in a reluctant and expensive reinsurance market. In addition, the problem of accurately determing the size of the portfolio can become quite complicated and costly.

The policies attaching method is another method of determining which risks will fall within the terms of the treaty. This is probably the most widely used method in the London market, as opposed to the premiums earned basis which is the most popular in the United States. Under the policies attaching basis, all policies which attach, or become effective, during the treaty year come within the terms of the treaty. If the agreement is cancelled at the end of the treaty year, the reinsurer remains at risk for all losses which occur under policies issued during the year until they all expire. This is known as the "run-off" of the treaty. The run-off may be as long as three to five years, depending upon the type of policy issued by the ceding company.

Under this method, the outgoing reinsurer has to maintain the unearned premium reserve for the duration of the run-off. Under the premiums earned basis, responsibility for maintenance of the unearned premium reserve is passed to the incoming reinsurer through the use of the portfolio.

The policies attaching basis is the most popular method in the marine area because the majority of the hulls are insured on an annual basis and attach on the first of January. The vast majority of the cargo policies issued are "voyage," i.e., they cover the cargo for the duration of the scheduled voyage to delivery. It is evident that the amount which spills over into the next year as run-off is relatively small, thus making the run-off factor relatively unimportant. Furthermore, the accounting under the policies attaching system is considerably less involved than under the premiums earned system. There is no need to worry about the size of the portfolio and of handling the various entries necessary to effect the transfer of the portfolio.

Loss Adjustment

The ceding company has full control over the settlement of claims. If the ceding company selects to compromise a claim, to reject it, or to contest it by legal proceedings, the reinsurer is obligated to share in its proportion of the loss and loss expense. This rule holds true even if the amount of settlement is increased because of the legal proceedings undertaken by the ceding company in an effort to refute the claim. If the ceding company makes an *ex gratia* settlement, the reinsurer is normally responsible for its proportion of the settlement. An *ex gratia* settlement is the payment of a claim even though the company is not strictly liable under the terms of the contract of insurance. Unless a clause is included in the treaty wording giving such wide latitude to the ceding company in the settlement of its claims, the reinsurer by common law may refute court costs and *ex gratia* payments unless its consent to such action is first obtained.

The reinsurer also shares in any salvage or recoveries in the same proportion as it shared in the claim. Loss adjustment clauses give the ceding company the freedom of action it needs in order to act immediately. Quick action is normally in the best interests of all parties concerned.

System of Accounts

Settlement under a treaty is normally by account. The ceding company periodically sends to the reinsurer a statement of account showing premiums collected for the period, returns and cancellations, paid losses, and adjustments in the outstanding claims reserve and the unearned premium reserve. Although the reinsurer is technically responsible for maintaining the reserves, often they remain within the coffers of the ceding company until earned. All of the debit and credit items will be balanced against each other, and the ceding company will enclose with the statement a check for the balance. In the United States, the normal practice is to have monthly statements with semi-annual and annual summaries; however, because of the cost of preparing such statements every month, many companies convert to quarterly statements of account if possible. European insurers normally use the quarterly system of account.

From the advent of the treaty until just a few years ago, the ceding company was required to submit forms which were known as bordereaux. Such a requirement is the exception rather than the rule in present day practice. A bordereau is a detailed statement of all risks ceded under the treaty during a definite period of time. It used to be a long typewritten statement which gave the policy number, the name of the insured, address, subject matter of insurance, and premium charged. With the introduction of the computer, the typewritten bordereaux were replaced with computer prepared statements.

The purpose of the bordereau was to allow the reinsurer to index its acceptances in just the same manner as the ceding company. By indexing the risks, the reinsurer could determine when it became too heavily committed in any one area. If such were the case, the reinsurer could reduce its liability by retroceding a portion to another reinsurer. The participation of Lloyd's, London, in the San Francisco Earthquake of 1906, is a good indication of how carefully this indexing was accomplished around the turn of the century. Lloyd's was acting as reinsurer for some insurers who experienced heavy losses. Lloyd's was able to assess with fair accuracy its share of the losses through its agents' estimates and to send checks for those amounts before the ceding companies themselves were able to accurately establish their losses.

Another use of the bordereau is as a checking device to ensure that the ceding company is biding by the terms of the treaty. With the omission of the bordereau, the reinsurer is no longer able to do this; therefore, a clause is included in the treaty wording which gives the reinsurer, or its representative, the power to inspect the books of the ceding company at any reasonable time.

The following list of bordereau is included in order to give the reader an idea of the many types of bordereau that can be required to be submitted by the ceding company: provisional claims bordereau, preliminary or provisional bordereau, definite bordereau, endorsement bordereau, definite claims bordereau, reinsurance bordereau, and reinsurance recoveries bordereau. It is evident that with the present-day volume of business, the costs of preparing and keeping track of each one of these bordereau exceeds the value of the information derived therefrom.

Reserves

One of the functions of treaty reinsurance is that it relieves the ceding company of the obligation of maintaining an unearned premium reserve on the portion of the liability ceded to the reinsurer. The treaty reinsurer becomes responsible for maintaining the unearned premium reserve. There are primarily two methods of arriving at the size of this reserve: (1) actual calculation of the unearned premium of each policy in the portfolio, and (2) the use of pro-rata fractions.

The actual calculation of the unearned premium on each policy in force is obviously the most accurate method. The figure obtained is the actual amount of unearned premiums at the time of the audit. It is also the most time consuming and costly method. Because of this fact, most insurers prefer to sacrifice a little accuracy and use one of the other methods in the interest of efficiency. In the actual calculation of unearned premiums, someone or something, must check each individual policy and calculate its unearned portion. By adding the results of all of the calculations, the unearned premium reserve for the entire portfolio is obtained. With the growing utilization of computers, such calculations are greatly facilitated. As a result, this method of calculating unearned premium reserves is growing in use.

The second method, the use of pro-rata fractions, is probably the most widely used in the United States. It yields a figure which is reasonably accurate in a relatively short series of calculations. The principle employed assumes that during normal operations, approximately the same number of policies will become effective every day. Thus, the average commencement date of all policies issued during any single month would be the 15th day. For example, the average commencement date of all policies issued in January, 1969, would be January 15, 1969. If all of the policies issued were for a period of one year, the average date of expiration for all of these policies would be 12:01 A.M. January 15, 1970. The premiums paid in by the insureds would be completely earned at that time. On June 15, 1969, according to this system, all of the policies issued in January will have been in force for half of their life; therefore, 50 percent of the premiums paid in would be earned. Following the same line of reasoning, as of the 15th of each month, the policies will be another 1/12th earned.

The statements are not due to the reinsurers, however, as of the 15th of each month, but rather on the first. The premium earned on the first of the month is one-half of one month's premium or 1/24th of the annual premium. These various fractions (1/12, 1/24, 1/36, etc.) are called the pro-rata fractions and are the basic fractions used in calculating the unearned premiums for this method.

Seldom does a property-liability insurer issue policies exclusively on an annual basis. Policies are also issued for a period of two, three, four, and five years. Only on infrequent occasions are policies issued for a period of two or four years. It has been found that for the purposes of the pro-rata fractions method, the premiums for the two and four year policies can be incorporated in either the one, three, or five year premiums in the interest of efficiency without sacrificing any degree of accuracy. If, however, there are a large number of two and four year policies, they should be figured individually. Following the same procedure as for the one year policies discussed above, the three year policies commencing in January, 1969, will be one-third earned on January 15, 1970, two-thirds earned on January 15, 1971, and fully earned on January 15, 1972. On the 15th of each month, they will be 1/36th earned; and on the first of the second month, February, they will be 1/72nd earned. Similarly, the five year policies commencing at the same time as the one and three year policies will be 1/5th earned on January 15, 1970, and fully earned on January 15, 1974, 1/120th being earned on February 1, 1969.

The following example is provided in order to illustrate how the computation of the unearned premium reserve is accomplished under the pro-rata fraction method. The percentage of premiums written each month by Company A is made up of approximately 60 percent one year term policies, 25 percent three year term policies, and 15 percent five year term policies. Company A's total monthly premium income for all three types of policies is $10,000, or $120,000 annual premium income. For ease of calculation, it is assumed that Company A started into business as of January 1, 1969. The calculations below represent those after one year's operation, i.e., on December 31, 1969.

The fraction unearned as of December 31, 1969, for those policies which expire in January, 1970, is 1/24th. Because the average expiration of all of the policies attaching in January is the 15th, there is one-half of one month's premium to yet be earned, or $250. Note on Table I that the total unearned premiums are one-half of the total net premiums for annual policies.

Under actual circumstances, the calculation is a little more complicated because of a growing premium volume. Thus, instead of showing a constant $6,000 monthly premium income on the annual policy, the figures will vary according to the seasons and due to the general growth of premium writing of the various terms of policies; for example, instead of one table for three year and five year policies, there would be three and five respectively.

Another reserve which is maintained is the outstanding claims re-

TABLE I

EARNED PREMIUM ON ONE YEAR POLICIES OF COMPANY A

POLICIES EXPIRING	TOTAL NET PREMIUM	FRACTION UNEARNED	UNEARNED PREMIUMS
January 1969	$ 6,000	1/24	$ 250
February 1969	6,000	3/24	750
March 1969	6,000	5/24	1,250
April 1969	6,000	7/24	1,750
May 1969	6,000	9/24	2,250
June 1969	6,000	11/24	2,750
July 1969	6,000	13/24	3,250
August 1969	6,000	15/24	3,750
September 1969	6,000	17/24	4,250
October 1969	6,000	19/24	4,750
November 1969	6,000	21/24	5,250
December 1969	6,000	23/24	5,750
BALANCE	$72,000		$36,000

TABLE II

EARNED PREMIUM ON THREE YEAR POLICIES OF COMPANY A

POLICIES EXPIRING	TOTAL NET PREMIUMS	FRACTION UNEARNED	UNEARNED PREMIUMS
January 1972	$ 2,500	49/72	$ 1,701
February 1972	2,500	51/72	1,770
March 1972	2,500	53/72	1,839
April 1972	2,500	55/72	1,909
May 1972	2,500	57/72	1,978
June 1972	2,500	59/72	2,048
July 1972	2,500	61/72	2,117
August 1972	2,500	63/72	2,187
September 1972	2,500	65/72	2,256
October 1972	2,500	67/72	2,326
November 1972	2,500	69/72	2,395
December 1972	2,500	71/72	2,465
BALANCE	$30,000		$24,991

TABLE III

EARNED PREMIUM ON FIVE YEAR POLICIES
OF COMPANY A

POLICIES EXPIRING	TOTAL NET PREMIUM	FRACTION UNEARNED	UNEARNED PREMIUMS
January 1974	$ 1,500	97/120	$ 1,212
February 1974	1,500	99/120	1,237
March 1974	1,500	101/120	1,262
April 1974	1,500	103/120	1,287
May 1974	1,500	105/120	1,312
June 1974	1,500	107/120	1,337
July 1974	1,500	109/120	1,362
August 1974	1,500	111/120	1,387
September 1974	1,500	113/120	1,412
October 1974	1,500	115/120	1,437
November 1974	1,500	117/120	1,462
December 1974	1,500	119/120	1,487
BALANCE	$18,000		$16,194

TABLE IV

UNEARNED PREMIUM RESERVE
OF COMPANY A

TOTAL NET PREMIUMS WRITTEN DECEMBER 31, 1969		$120,000
Unearned Premium Reserve for Annual Policies	$36,000	
Unearned Premium Reserve for 3 Year Policies .	24,991	
Unearned Premium Reserve for 5 Year Policies .	16,194	
TOTAL UNEARNED PREMIUM RESERVE		77,185
TOTAL PREMIUMS EARNED, 1969		$ 42,815

serve. This is a reserve composed of the estimates of the probable size of losses that are known but for some reason are not settled. As each loss is finally settled, the reserve is adjusted accordingly until all known losses have been settled to the satisfaction of both parties.

It is often the practice, particularly when the reinsurer is domiciled in a foreign country, for the ceding company to maintain a premium reserve. This reserve is not to be confused with the Unearned Premium Reserve. The purpose of the premium reserve is to ensure that the reinsurer meets its obligations. The premium reserve is expressed as a percentage of the premiums ceded during the period, generally 40 percent, and is released after being held for an agreed period, normally one year. The reinsurer is paid an agreed percentage interest in order to partially compensate it for interest it loses by not having possession of the funds during the period.

Period of a Treaty and Cancellation Provisions

The treaty becomes effective as of a certain date, and all insurances issued or renewed after that date are automatically ceded to the reinsurer as stipulated in the contract. The treaty normally continues in force indefinitely until cancelled by either party.

There are primarily two ways a treaty may be cancelled: (1) by either party exercising its option, or (2) automatic cancellation as a result of some extraneous cause. In the former case, the normal procedure is to provide that either party may cancel the contract at the end of any treaty year by giving ninety days written notice. On occasion, a provision calling for six months or 180 days notice is encountered, however, such provisions are uncommon.

A treaty may be automatically cancelled under two circumstances, war or a significant change in the financial strength of the reinsurer. If war, declared or undeclared, breaks out between the countries in which the parties to the treaty are residing, carrying on business, or incorporated, the treaty is automatically cancelled. A "War Clause" normally provides that the *entire* liability of the reinsurer shall cease as of the date of the outbreak of war. The automatic termination of all liability is designed to avoid possible confusion surrounding the reinsurer's liability for previous cessions. Confusion and possible disagreement is avoided by providing for immediate cancellation of all liability on the part of either party. This brings to light another reason for the premium reserve requirement when dealing between countries. The ceding company might not otherwise receive a refund of the unearned portion of the premiums from the reinsurer since it is in a beligerent country. If it has in its possession a premium reserve approximately equal to the unearned premiums held in the reinsurer's account, a possibly difficult situation is avoided.

A treaty may also be automatically cancelled by the ceding company if at any time the reinsurer should (1) lose the whole or any part of its paid-up capital, or (2) go into liquidation or have a receiver appointed, or (3) be acquired by or have control shifted to any other company. The above provisions constitute what is known as the "Sudden Death Clause." It is intended to allow the ceding company to cancel the contract immediately if the financial structure of the reinsurer is weakened or appreciably altered. The purpose of the Sudden Death Clause is easily understood, for such changes impair or could impair the reinsurer's ability to meet its contractural obligations. The cancellation is effective immediately in order to avoid the situation in which the reinsurer is in receivership or dire financial straits, and the ceding company is required by contract to continue making cessions to the reinsurer until the outherwise required notice period has expired.

Sometimes this clause is broadened so as to provide for immediate cancellation, without notice, if the currency of either country is devalued, or its free transferability is restricted by government decree. The object of such a provision is to prevent either party from being unduly prejudiced by a sudden devaluation of the currency or by restrictions being placed upon its export. Again, the theoretical basis for this provision is that the situation surrounding the agreement has been altered to the extent that neither party is assured that the contract requirements can be satisfied as originally intended.

Arbitration

Invariably, treaties provide for settlement of disputes between parties through arbitration. There are minor variations between the arbitration clauses, however, they all have basically the same characteristics. First, each party is to appoint an arbitrator. Before they start arbitration proceedings, the arbitrators appoint an umpire. The actual decision by the court of arbitration is made by the arbitrators, if they are able to agree. In the event they are unable to agree, the umpire is called into action; and it becomes his responsibility to make the final decision. Thirty days is the normal period allowed for the appointment of arbitrators after notification by one party of the desire to take a dispute into arbitration. The arbitrators appointed must be responsible executives of property-liability insurance companies who are in no way connected with either of the disputing parties. If one party fails to appoint an arbitrator within the prescribed time, the other party may appoint the second arbitrator and proceed in the normal fashion.

Contract interpretation, as an honorable rather than as a strictly legal agreement, is a second common characteristic found in the arbitration clause. The Court of Arbitration is released from all judicial formality and is not required to follow the strict word of the law. The arbitrators should settle the dispute according to an equitable, rather than strictly legal, interpretation of the terms of the agreement. This brings out the reason behind having the court made up of insurance executives from companies in the same field. They are in a better position to accurately interpret the contract in light of current practices and customs in the market. As a result, the true intentions of the parties when they entered the agreement should prevail rather than their being overcome because of some technical defect in the contract itself. By having such a provision, both parties are trying to ensure that the intent of the agreement be carried out.

The decision reached by the court is binding on both parties. Arbitration on agreements carried out in the United States come within the terms of the Federal Arbitration Act (U.S.C.A.' tit. 9), and awards made under it may be vacated upon application by one of the parties to the arbitration only in the following instances:

> (A) Where the award was procured by corruption, fraud or undue means. (B) Where there was evident partiality or corruption in the arbitrators, or either of them. (C) Where the arbitrators were guilty of misconduct in refusing to postpone the hearing, upon sufficient cause shown, or in refusing to hear evidence pertinent and material to the controversy; or of any other misbehavior by which the rights of any party have been prejudiced. (D) Where the arbitrators exceed their powers, or so imperfectly executed them that a mutual, final and definite award upon the subject matter submitted was not made. (E) Where an award is vacated and the time within which the agreement required the award to be made has not expired, the court may, in its discretion, direct a rehearing by the arbitrators.[2]

Each party is to pay the expenses of its own arbitrator, and the costs of the umpire are to be borne equally by both parties. If one party failed to appoint an arbitrator resulting in the other party appointing both, the costs of arbitration are to be shared equally between parties just as though each had appointed an arbitrator as provided in the contract.

General Functions of Automatic Pro-Rata Reinsurance Treaties

Treaty reinsurance was developed to facilitate the efficient handling of a large volume of reinsurance transactions. As a consequence, it is designed to allow an automatic increase in the ceding company's underwriting capacity. Larger lines on each risk can be accepted by the underwriter because of the guarantee of reinsurance coverage on an automatic basis.

Because there is definite, traceable cession of liability on each individual risk, the responsibility for the maintenance of the unearned premium reserves on the portion of the liability ceded is also transferred to the reinsurer. Unearned premium reserve relief is the basis for the "banking" function offered to the primary insurer under treaty reinsurance. The reinsurer helps finance a young company's growth by providing a method for the insurer to release its equity

[2]K. R. Thompson, *Reinsurance.* (Philadelphia: Chilton Co., 1951), p. 110.

tied up in the unearned premium reserves. By assuming responsibility for a portion of the reserve and paying the ceding company a reinsurance commission, the reinsurer furnishes funds to the ceding company to finance further growth.

CHAPTER SUMMARY

Automatic pro-rata reinsurance may be defined as an obligatory reinsurance agreement between parties, so that the ceding company is bound to cede and the reinsurer is bound to accept the share of the risks to be reinsured as provided in the treaty. Such reinsurance agreements are proportional reinsurances because the reinsurer and the ceding company share in a fixed proportion the premiums, liability, and claims on risks which come within the terms of the treaty.

The following are the common characteristics of all types of pro-rata treaties. (1) The liability of the reinsurer commences simultaneously with that of the ceding company. (2) The premiums received by the reinsurer are the ones paid by the original insured. (3) The ceding company is paid a reinsurance commission which is designed to cover its acquisition expenses, premium taxes, and the costs of servicing the business. (4) The reinsurer follows the settlements of the ceding company on any claims which arise under the insurances covered by the treaty. (5) The treaty is normally for an indefinite period and may be cancelled at the option of either party upon giving three months written notice. The treaty is automatically cancelled in the event of war between the country in which the reinsurer is domiciled and the country in which the ceding company is domiciled, or in the event of a significant change in the financial structure of the reinsurer. (6) In the event of a disagreement, the dispute is referred to arbitration rather than to the courts for a decision which is binding upon both parties.

There are three basic functions common to every type of treaty. They provide the ceding company automatic reinsurance on every risk insured within the applicable classes. They increase the ceding company's capacity to accept greater liability. They finance growth through unearned premium reserve assumption by the reinsurer.

The two types of treaties under which the vast bulk of pro-rata reinsuring is performed, are the surplus and the quota share treaties. Of these two, the surplus treaty is the more prominent in reinsurance affairs. The surplus treaty is an automatic reinsurance agreement whereby the reinsurer is bound to accept, and the ceding company is bound to cede only the surplus liability in excess of a predetermined limit. This limit is known as the retention. Because of the retention, the surplus treaty is especially useful to the ceding company for the establishment of size homogeneity. It has the disadvantage, however, of being more costly to administer than the quota share treaty.

The quota share treaty may be defined as an automatic reinsurance agreement whereby the ceding company is bound to cede, and the reinsurer is bound to accept a fixed percentage of every risk written by the ceding company on an agreed class of business. Quota share reinsurance passes on to the reinsurer business on the same basis as it is received by the ceding company. This is the basis for the primary disadvantage of this type of treaty as far as the primary insurer is concerned. The ceding company passes on to the reinsurer a large amount of the profits which probably would be retained under any other type of treaty.

Because of the high cost, the quota share treaty is utilized for special purposes to which the other types of pro-rata agreements are not well suited. The services which it performs for the primary insurer are (1) to finance the growth of a small company, (2) to finance surplus, (3) to spread the risk upon entry into a new geographical area or line of business, and (4) to support a weak member of a group of companies.

The facultative obligatory treaty is designed to allow the ceding company to place its more standardized facultative risks on an automatic basis, thereby reducing its administration costs. The facultative obligatory treaty is an automatic reinsurance agreement whereby the ceding company is at its option to cede, and the reinsurer is bound to accept a share of certain defined risks underwritten by the ceding company.

Among the special types of treaties which are designed to perform relatively specialized tasks, the retrocession agreement and portfolio reinsurance are of particular importance. A retrocession is the term used to describe the reinsuring of liability assumed through reinsurance. Although a retrocession agreement may take any of the various forms of reinsurance, it is most commonly found in the form of a quota share treaty. Portfolio reinsurance is the reinsuring of a block of direct business by the primary insurer. This is normally done in three situations: (1) in a treaty transfer from one reinsurer to another, (2) in order to immediately withdraw from a geographical area or class of business, and (3) in order to increase the year end ratio of surplus to unearned premium reserve.

CHAPTER IV

Excess Reinsurance

THE EXCESS METHOD of reinsuring grew out of the need on the part of the primary insurer for a catastrophe or high limit reinsurance coverage of some sort. The purpose of the high loss protection is to limit the insurer's maximum possible loss in any one event to a relatively definite amount. By definitely limiting its maximum loss, the insurer effectively protects its annual loss ratio from shock losses which might seriously threaten its financial strength or diminish the attractiveness of its stock to investors. Excess reinsurance is the youngest form of reinsurance, having been developed by Mr. Cuthbert Heath of Lloyd's, London, in the 1880's.[1] *The excess* form of reinsurance did not start being widely used until the early 1920's. Just as the automatic pro-rata treaty largely replaced the facultative reinsurance, the excess form is increasingly absorbing what has previously been considered the domain of the treaty. This replacement will not be so complete, however, as that of the treaty-facultative evolution because of the wide difference in characteristics of the excess and treaty which is not present in the facultative-treaty reinsurances. As will be reflected throughout the following discussion, the excess form of reinsurance represents a vast simplification in procedure over the facultative and treaty forms. The simplification has enabled a substantial reduction in reinsurance handling costs to the primary insurer.

Since excess of loss reinsurance is the mainstay of the excess form, the following discussion of the basic characteristics of the excess form is in terms of the excess of loss contract. Later in the chapter, the other types of excess reinsurance are examined and any variations from the characteristics of excess of loss is then brought forward.

[1]Kenneth R. Thompson, *Reinsurance* (Philadelphia: Chilton Co., 1951), p. 34.

EXCESS REINSURANCE, A DEFINITION

Excess reinsurance may be defined as a reinsurance agreement whereby the reinsurer agrees to reimburse the ceding company for all losses, or a large portion thereof, over a relatively high limit (the net retention), for consideration of a percentage of the ceding company's net premium income. Under this form of reinsurance, the reinsurer does not become interested in a loss until it has exceeded the net retention. Once the net retention has been exceeded, the reinsurer pays the entirety of the excess amount of loss up to its limit of liability; the loss then reverts back to the ceding company. There may be an element of co-insurance in the coverage. The reinsurer may not be liable for the entirety of the excess, but rather a very large percentage, e.g., 90 percent. Excess reinsurance may work as in the following example. The ceding company's net retention is $50,000, and the excess coverage extends for another $100,000 (such a coverage is expressed as $100,000 excess of $50,000). If a loss amounting to $90,000 is experienced, the ceding company would pay the first $50,000, and the reinsurer would pay the remaining $40,000. If, in this same situation, the loss were $170,000, the ceding company would pay the first $50,000, the reinsurer the next $100,000; the balance, $20,000, would revert back to the ceding company.

Excess of loss reinsurance will be contrasted with treaty reinsurance as a method of introducing the investigation of the excess of loss form. This discussion has a dual purpose: (1) to act as a reference point for the discussion of excess reinsurance, and (2) to put forward the semantic plea that the forms of excess reinsurance should not be called "treaties" (e.g., excess of loss treaty), but rather excess of loss "contracts" or some other applicable word. The historical reason for calling the excess forms of reinsurance "treaties" is probably a result of these contracts being handled by the treaty department during their early development. There are, however, distinct differences between the two forms which require recognition and justify their separate identities. The following tabular summary of the differences is presented to facilitate an easy comparison of the two forms.

In the treaty form, the reinsurer accepts a proportionate share of the liability of the ceding company. It is, therefore, financially interested in every premium payment and every claim settlement made to or by the ceding company. In the excess form, however, the reinsurer is not sharing any proportionate liability but stands alone on losses after they exceed the net retention.

The premium paid to the treaty reinsurer is a percentage of the

TABLE V
A SUMMARY OF THE DIFFERENCES BETWEEN
AUTOMATIC PRO-RATA TREATY AND EXCESS REINSURANCE

TREATY	EXCESS
a. Sharing agreement.	a. Individual liability.
b. Rate is original premium less commission.	b. Separate rate calculated by reinsurer.
c. Settlement by account.	c. Cash settlement.
d. Applies to specific risks.	d. Applies to the whole section of business.
e. Reinsurance commission given to ceding company.	e. No reinsurance commission given because ceding company is the insured.

premium paid by the insured. The reinsurance premium is in the same proportion as is the amount of liability ceded to the face of the policy. In excess reinsurance, the premium paid by the ceding company is calculated by the reinsurer, independent of the premium charged the insured. The treaty reinsurer gives its ceding company a reinsurance commission, whereas the excess reinsurer does not, as the ceding company is actually the insured.

The treaty covers the cession of a volume of individual risks; the liability on each risk insured can be directly traced to the reinsurer. Excess reinsurance covers a whole section of business, not applying to any specific risks, but only to losses which exceed the net retention. This is the reason treaty reinsurance is capable of relieving the ceding company of the burden of maintaining an unearned premium reserve on the portion of the liability ceded. On the other hand, the primary insurer finds no unearned premium reserve relief in the use of excess reinsurance. Finally, settlements under the treaty are by account; and settlements under the excess form are in cash within a relatively short period after notice of loss is received by the reinsurer. Because of these distinctions, excess forms of reinsurance are referred to in this chapter and throughout the book as "contracts." It is hoped that this will avoid any possible confusion in terminology and give excess reinsurance the individual identity it deserves.

CHARACTERISTICS OF EXCESS OF LOSS REINSURANCE

In addition to the previously discussed characteristics, there are several others which enable excess of loss reinsurance to function effectively as a vehicle for the absorption of losses in excess of a defined amount. These characteristics as discussed here are a result of various clauses comprising the contract, an example of which is included in Appendix A. Basic to the proper working of the excess of loss contract are the mechanics of establishing how a loss is to be counted, computed, and adjusted in order to accurately determine the reinsurer's liability. These "mechanics" are outlined by the ultimate net loss and associated clauses.

Ultimate Net Loss

Because the reinsurer becomes interested in only those losses which exceed the net retention, a definition of ultimate net loss is necessary. The ultimate net loss has to exceed the net retention before the reinsurer becomes interested in the loss. It is not just the loss "from the ground up," i.e., the total loss experienced by the insured. The ultimate net loss is normally defined as:

> The sum or sums paid in the settlement of all losses arising out of one event including any litigation or other expenses incurred in connection therewith, but excluding any charge for the services of any salaried employee of the ceding company in connection with the investigation of claims, and after deduction of all recoveries in respect of salvages or otherwise, and all sums recoverable under other reinsurances which inure to the benefit of this agreement.

The ultimate net loss is computed as follows: from the total amount of the loss, including the costs of litigation but not including salaries of employees, is deducted (1) recoveries from all underlying reinsurers, and (2) any salvage realized from the remains of the insured property. By using the ultimate net loss, the excess reinsurer is hoping to accurately ascertain the amount of loss only to the ceding company. Not included in this figure is the amount of loss to the underlying reinsurers, if any.

There are several factors in the preceding definition which bare further investigation, the first of these being "one event," or as it is often stated, "any one event." The importance of clearly understanding what normally constitutes "any one event" is self-evident. It is often upon the determination of this factor that the liability for payment depends. By carefully setting out what constitutes any one event, the contract protects the ceding company against heavy losses arising out of any one accident or occurrence or series of accidents or occurrences arising out of any one event. The excess reinsurer thus covers the ceding company's liability arising out of the Doctrine of

Proximate Cause, among other things; for it is intended to cover the liability for losses due to the same cause. In instances of an automobile accident, relatively little difficulty is experienced in determining a loss's applicability to the contract. The occurrence is usually well defined, and the resulting losses can be fairly easily determined. However, many third party claims can present a difficult problem, particularly in relation to the hazards of food poisoning or products liability.

Another area of possible difficulty in identifying a single loss is that of the "Acts of God," such as earthquake, flood, hail, and windstorm. In the flood area, the river basin or watershed basis is applied. Flood losses in an individual river basin or watershed are considered to constitute one event (flood). In excess of loss settlements covering losses due to hail storms, the difficulty arises when a distinction is sought concerning just where one hailstorm ends and another begins, i.e., what constitutes one occurrence. The normal practice is either to define the single occurrence as the losses which occur within a single twenty-four or a similar period, or all of the losses in a specific area such as a county. If the twenty-four hour basis is used, the ceding company is given the right to specify just exactly when the twenty-four hour period starts for loss purposes. On windstorms, tornadoes, and the like, all losses attributable to a single storm are considered to constitute one event.

Another factor which is reflected in the ultimate net loss clause is the liability of the reinsurer for expenses incurred by the ceding company in the settlement of a claim. In the clause quoted earlier, the reinsurer has given the ceding company a free hand in the settlement of claims. It may contest a claim if it so desires without consulting the reinsurer. The effect of this provision is that the reinsurer may become liable for a portion of a loss which it would not have had had the ceding company chosen to agree to the demands of the insured rather than to litigate. Recognizing this fact, reinsurers often insert a provision like this in the ultimate net loss clause: "An ultimate net loss as used herein shall be defined as the sum or sums paid in the settlement of all losses arising out of one event including any litigation expenses if incurred with the consent of the reinsurer . . ." If such a provision is included in the ultimate net loss clause and the ceding company litigates without first obtaining the reinsurer's consent, the reinsurer may refuse payment. "A defense can be based upon the fact that the underwriters did not consent, and this defense may be successful when they are sued for such expenses."[2] In such instances, the normal procedure is for the ceding company to

[2] *Ibid.*, p. 134.

avoid all difficulties which may arise as a result of this provision by first getting the consent of the reinsurer before starting litigation on any claims which stand the remotest chance of exceeding its net retention.

The ultimate net loss clause invariably includes a provision concerning salvage and other recoveries. The theory behind this provision is that any such recoveries reduce the amount of net loss to the ceding company. Since the excess reinsurer assumes all of the loss in excess of the net retention, the amount of recoveries should be deducted from the "top" of the loss pile, rather than the middle or below the net retention.

The way salvage apportionment works is well illustrated by a pair of example losses using an excess of loss contract having limits of $100,000 excess of $50,000. Losses A and B amount to $100,000 and $170,000, respectively. Since these two losses, both marine hulls, were constructive total losses, salvage was recovered amounting to $25,000 in both cases, thanks to Gillett Company. The recoveries from Loss A would all be applied to the ultimate net loss, thereby reducing the amount the reinsurer would have to pay by $25,000. If the reinsurer had already settled, which probably would be the case, the entire $25,000 would be refunded to the reinsurer. The recoveries from Loss B would be applied to the ultimate net loss, thereby reducing the loss to $145,000, $95,000 of which the reinsurer would have to pay. If the reinsurer had already settled for his maximum liability of $100,000, $5,000 would be refunded.

Loss B discloses a characteristic of this form of reinsurance in action. If the loss exceeds the reinsurer's maximum liability, the balance reverts back to the ceding company. Loss B went up through the net retention, continued on through the depth of the excess of loss coverage and, upon flowing out the top, reverted back to the ceding company for the remaining $20,000. Since the ceding company's additional $20,000 is on top of the loss-pile, so to speak, the salvage is first applied to it. The salvage works its way progressively down the loss until it is totally exhausted.

There is mention in the example ultimate net loss clause of deducting "all sums recoverable under other reinsurances which inure to the benefit of this agreement." This is frequently expressed as "all sums recoverable under underlying reinsurances." The intent of this provision is to ensure that the excess reinsurer is covering only the ceding company's exposure, its net retention, and not also that of the treaty, or underlying reinsurer's, unless it is the intent of the contract to do so.

Since the excess of loss contract applies only to the net retention, why is the loss not just assigned to the excess of loss contract once it exceeds the value of the net retention? For example, if the loss were $60,000 and the net retention $50,000, why should not the $10,000 be assigned to the excess reinsurer? A little reflection concerning the nature of a treaty answers this question and furnishes the key for the reason underlying reinsurances are deducted in ascertaining the ultimate net loss. Treaties are also known as proportional reinsurances because the ceding company and the treaty reinsurers share in every loss, no matter how small, in the same proportion as they share in the premiums and liabilities. If in the example above, the treaty were a ten line surplus with a retention of $20,000, and the loss were a total one, the amount of liability initially ceded to the treaty would have been $40,000, or $4,000 per line. The ceding company's retained liability is $20 000 instead of $50,000. It is evident that the ceding company would have to have more than two and one-half such risks destroyed in a single event in order to recover from the excess reinsurer.

In order to ensure that both parties understand the underlying reinsurance provision, sometimes an additional clarifying clause is included in the contract. It is known as the Net Retained Lines Clause. Such a clause might read something like this: "This reinsurance applies only to that portion of any insurance and/or reinsurance which the ceding company retains net for its own account, and in calculating the amount of any loss here under, only losses in respect of that portion of any insurance and/or reinsurance which the ceding company retains net for its own account shall be included."

Two further areas need to be considered before closing the discussion of the ultimate net loss clause. First, what is the liability of the excess reinsurer if an underlying reinsurer should fail to meet its portion of the loss? Secondly, when are settlements of a claim made under the excess contract? The ceding company is responsible to the insured for payment of the claim, not the reinsurers. The failure of a reinsurer to pay its portion of a loss, in essence, becomes the ceding company's loss until it can collect from the defaulting reinsurer. Does the failure of the reinsurer add to the ceding company's net loss and, therefore, become the liability of the excess reinsurer? Such a loss is not the same loss as the original loss. It is a loss due to another hazard, default of a reinsurer, rather than the hazard covered by the reinsurance, such as fire or third party liability. Therefore, the added loss to the ceding company because of a defaulting reinsurer does not come within the terms of the excess contract. The ceding company is solely responsible for selection of a reinsurer and for losses due to the hazard of financial default or failure of a reinsurer. In order to avoid any misunderstanding in this area, such a provision as the following is normally inserted into the contract: "It is understood and agreed that the amount of the reinsurer's liability hereunder in respect to any loss or losses shall not be increased by reason of the inability of the ceding company to collect from any other reinsurers, whether specific or general, any amounts which may have become due from them, whether such inability arises from the insolvency of such other reinsurers or otherwise."

Secondly, in many cases, the lapse of time between the loss, final settlement, recoveries, and salvages is a number of years. During this time, the ceding company could possibly become technically insolvent before it could recover from its excess reinsurer, if it were required to accurately determine its ultimate net loss prior to recovery. The excess of loss contract is designed to give the primary insurer an immediate source of funds. This is the reason for cash instead of account settlements. A provision is invariably included in the ultimate net loss clause setting out that the reinsurer is liable for its share of the *estimated* ultimate net loss, the fine adjustments to be made when the final results are in and analyzed. Such a provision often takes the following form: "Nothing, however, in this clause shall be construed as meaning that losses are not recovered hereunder until the ultimate net loss of the ceding company has been ascertained."

The above provision enables the ceding company to call upon the reinsurer for cash when a loss is experienced which it estimates will involve the excess reinsurer. The excess reinsurer becomes liable to pay the estimated amount, in cash, within a relatively short period of time. As the actual amount of loss becomes known, the excess reinsurer may be called on to pay a little more, or receive a refund, as the case may be.

Class Coverage

Excess of loss reinsurance is designed to function as excess coverage for a line of business. It covers all policies issued in respect to a certain line of business without regard to the individual policies issued thereunder. Excess of loss coverage is often referred to as "Blanket" reinsurance because of the natural extension of this coverage from the protection of a single line to two or more lines. What might be considered the ultimate in this extension is the Umbrella Coverage which could accurately be called a "super-blanket" excess of loss contract, for it is designed to cover all classes of business the ceding company writes as the sole reinsurance coverage. Because of this broad coverage of any losses in the line, the primary insurer is ensured of having protection with a minimum of clerical work and other administrative expense.

Exclusions

As with any contract of insurance or reinsurance, there are exclusions which limit the liability of the reinsurer with respect to certain types of risks. The specific exclusions vary from line to line of business written by the primary insurer; however, no matter what class an excess of loss contract is covering, two general areas will be excluded. First, all of the exclusions listed generally will relate to classes of risks in which the catastrophe hazard is prevalent. In these risks, the chance of heavy loss is considerably above normal. This does not mean that the ceding company may not cover such risks under its excess of loss contract, someone has to cover them. The ceding company may include such risks under its contract if it first obtains permission from the reinsurer to do so. The ceding company who makes a practice of regularly insuring this type of risk may negotiate a contract which does not exclude them. It should be writing a sufficient volume to yield an adequate spread, thus making its losses relatively predictable. To these insurers, this type of risk is not extra hazardous but rather yields high premium insurance. It is the primary insurer who writes such risks only on occasion, normally to accommodate an agent or broker, who is excluded from covering them under its excess of loss contract. These insurers are not writing a sufficient volume in order to obtain an adequate spread, and they probably are not charging an adequate rate.

Secondly, a common exclusion in both treaty and excess reinsurance agreements is that of reinsurances accepted by the ceding company on an excess of loss basis. Both of these forms often cover the ceding company for reinsurance accepted on a treaty or sharing basis but never on an excess basis. The reason for this exclusion is easy to understand. The treaty premium is fixed as a percentage of the original premium paid by the insured to cover the chance of loss incurred by the insurer for issuing insurance coverage. Excess of loss reinsurance rates are also expressed as a percentage of the total original premium received by the ceding company, but at a rate which would be inadequate for the risk accepted under a treaty form. For example, Ceding Company A obtains excess of loss coverage from Reinsurer X for losses in excess of $5,000 at a rate of 8 percent of its original premium. Ceding Company A also accepts an excess of loss contract from Ceding Company B for losses in excess of $3,000 for a rate of 10 percent. If this excess liability from Company B accepted by Company A were reinsurable under its contract with Reinsurer X, it would mean that at a rate of 8 percent of 10 percent, or eight-tenths of one percent, Reinsurer X is accepting liability for Ceding Company B's losses in excess of $8,000 ($3,000 retained by B, and $5,000 retained by A). If an excess of $3,000 is worth 10 percent, it can hardly be stated that an excess of $8,000 is worth only 0.8 percent. For this reason, all excess reinsurances accepted by the ceding company are excluded under the contract.

Rating Methods — Excess of Loss

The premium, or rate, for an excess of loss contract is normally expressed as a percentage of the gross net premium income written by the ceding company for the line or class covered. Gross net premium income (GNPI) is equal to the gross premium written, less returns, cancellations, bonuses (dividends), and premiums of reinsurances which reduce the exposure to the contract concerned (underlying reinsurances). Because of the earned premium system in the United States, one occasionally finds GNPI expressed as the Gross Net Earned Premium Income. In essence, this means the reported earned premium income of the ceding company, since in figuring the amount of earned premiums, the items deducted above are also deducted. Since the vast bulk of excess of loss reinsurance for insurers in the United States was placed in London until the mid 1950's, the normal expression is gross net premium income.

The purpose of using the GNPI as the base upon which to apply the rate is to obtain the true net premium income retained by the ceding company for its own account. It is the retained liability which the excess is protecting. The one obvious exception to using the reinsured's gross net premium income is in the use of the excess coverage to protect its treaty reinsurers, or "for common account" as it is called. When the excess is for common account, the rate is applied to the gross net premium income ceded to the treaty reinsurers. The treaty GNPI is equal to the gross premium ceded, less returns, cancellations, bonuses, and the premium paid for the excess coverage.

The calculation of the rate presents a problem of sizable proportions. It is not possible to lay down any table of rates which can be consulted to set an actuarially sound rate, such as is attempted in primary insurance rates. The varying conditions which surround the liability covered are so fluid that the rate set today may well be inaccurate tomorrow; consequently, a rating method must be used which can float, to a degree, with the changing exposure. Several general factors affect the rate, the primary ones being (1) the level of the net retention and the limit of liability of the reinsurer; (2) the range of business and whether the contract embodies the normal exclusions;

(3) the past experience of the ceding company; and (4) the underwriting limits of the ceding company.

Basic to the determination of the rate is the level of the ceding company's net retention and the reinsurer's limit of liability. The lower the net retention, the larger the number of claims the reinsurer can expect to exceed it, and, therefore, the higher will be the rate. The greater the reinsurer's limit of liability, the greater is its exposure, and, therefore, the higher will be the rate. The difficulty arises in determining just how much more should be charged with each successive drop in the level of the retention and each successive increase in the limits. It is not possible to say that an excess of $5,000 costs twice as much as an excess of $10,000. Because of the larger number of smaller policies issued, the probability is that more than twice the number of losses will exceed $5,000 than $10,000; but just exactly how many, or to what extent, is largely undeterminable.

Secondly, the range of business covered, as well as the number of exclusions in the contract, affects the rate. If the contract covers several classes of risks, some subject to heavy losses to a greater degree than others, the coverage will probably cost more than if it covered one very limited area. If a number of the normal exclusions were eliminated from the contract through negotiation, the ceding company could expect to pay more; for the risk assumed by the reinsurer is greater than if all of the exclusions remained intact.

The effects of the two considerations above will vary from insurer to insurer because of their different underwriting policies and general areas served. In recognition of this fact, the excess underwriter places a great deal of weight on the past experience of the proposing company. The past experience is probably a good indication of the amount of exposure the reinsurer will undertake at the various levels of net retention being considered. The proposing company will supply figures covering a period of years displaying its annual net premium income for each year and the number and cost of all claims which have exceeded the proposed net retention. From these figures, it is a simple matter to determine what the pure cost of this coverage over the period involved would have been had the proposed contract been inforce during that time. The total amount of claims in excess of the net retention, divided by the number of years in the period, yields the actual average cost of paying the claims which would have arisen under the coverage. This figure is the "pure cost" of the coverage. The pure cost is often referred to as the Burning Cost to the reinsurer, for if the reinsurer had charged less than this amount, the losses would have exceeded the premium income. A loading is added to the pure cost which is designed to cover three items: (1) the reinsurer's cost of operations, (2) the profit to the reinsurer for offering the coverage, and (3) the maintenance of a surplus with which to absorb the wide fluctuations in experience characteristic of this coverage.

Probably the most difficult task for the reinsuring underwriter is to establish a rate which is adequate to perform the tasks outlined above and yet not be exorbitant in the eyes of the reinsured. The difficulty is due to the basic function of this coverage, i.e., to protect the reinsured against the wide fluctuations in experience. In order to do this, the excess reinsurer has to absorb these fluctuations. The only way they can be absorbed without periodically shaking the reinsurer's financial structure is for it to charge a rate which will not only cover the costs of offering the service but which will also establish and maintain a surplus. The problem of having an adequate surplus is negligible so far as the majority of the claims are concerned, for they will be small enough for the reinsurer to meet out of its current premium income. However, since the limits of liability on excess of loss contracts sometimes reach stupendous proportions, occasional losses of catastrophic nature occur which have to be absorbed by this surplus.

As a consequence of the wide variation in experience which it can expect from a single account, the excess reinsurer normally attempts to obtain a large number of contracts and limit its commitment on any one account to such proportions as to yield a relatively stable and, therefore, predictable loss ratio. It naturally follows that in order for the reinsurer to establish a surplus, the reinsurer must be reasonably assured that the primary insurer shall continue the contract for a relatively long period of time.

The surplus problem for the reinsuring underwriter is further compounded by the fact of negotiation. In direct insurance, the insured in the vast majority of cases does not even consider the idea of negotiating a rate. By setting its own rate for insurance it issues, the primary insurer can be assured, to a certain degree, of periodically increasing its surplus. The excess reinsurer is allowed no such luxury. Negotiation is the password throughout reinsurance, and the rate is not exempt. When the ceding company experiences a good year, it expects the reinsurer to lower the rate as a reflection of this favorable turn of events. If the rate is lowered, the periodic building of the surplus is obviously slowed down. If, on the other hand, the experience is poor, the excess reinsurer immediately adjusts the rate upward to compensate for this increase in losses at the end of the contract year.

If continuity were a fact, i.e., the fact of renewal, a level premium could probably be charged which would allow for this gradual building and maintenance of a surplus and put an end to this constant negotiation. The theory is fine. Because of human nature, however, such will probably never be the case in practice; so the best action is to learn to survive as others have done in the past. The other alternative, to go down in a blaze of glory while clutching to high theoretical ideals, is a worthy thought but appears rather impractical.

The excess underwriter has found that the last five years' experience yields a more accurate estimation of the immediate future results than would the consideration of the last ten, fifteen, or twenty years. This is primarily due to three factors: (1) the ever increasing value of the average sum insured as a result of big business practices, (2) inflation, and (3) the ever increasing size of jury awards. All of these factors have contributed to the rise in the number of losses which exceed a particular level of retention.

The method of rating being generally described above is the Burning Cost Method. Burning cost is probably the most widely used rating method because it yields a figure which is reasonably accurate and easy to compute. Briefly, the burning cost method determines the rate for an excess of loss coverage by first establishing the pure cost of the coverage, i.e., the total amount of losses exceeding the proposed net retention during the period. The pure cost is divided by the number of years comprising the experience period, normally five years, yielding the average pure cost per year, or annual "burning" cost. A loading is applied to the burning cost to cover the reinsurer's cost of operation, to establish a surplus for heavy losses, and to yield a profit to the reinsurer.

The loading may be expressed as a percentage or as a fraction. In the ocean marine area, the percentage figure appears to predominate at this time, the loading varying anywhere from 25 percent to 33⅓ percent, depending upon the quality of the past experience. In the non-ocean marine areas, the loading expressed as a fraction is encountered with greater regularity, the fraction varying anywhere from 100/60 for an exceptionally poor account and/or high retention, to 100/75 for an exceptionally good account and/or low retention. The vast bulk of the fractions applied range around 100/65 to 100/70.

It is difficult to set down any reason for the variation in the expression of the loading, for both could be expressed as a percentage and yield the same results. However, because of the high percentage of loading encountered at times, a case might be made for the fraction being used as a diversion in order to mask, to a degree, the percentage of loading being applied. For example, a loading of 100/60 is equal to 66⅔ percent, while 100/65 yields a percentage loading of 53.9 percent. If such a loading were expressed in a percentage form, the primary insurer might well balk during the negotiations when the rate is mentioned. This is not to say that the loading is grossly out of proportion (although it might be), but rather to point out that the loading expressed as a fraction might tend to cushion the psychological effect of the high cost.

The reason for the higher loading in the non-ocean marine fields as opposed to the marine field is the greater variation in experience and the greater size of the possible catastrophic loss which can be expected. The difference in possible losses between the two areas can be appreciated when one considers the possibility of three or more vessels insured by the same ceding company, or by ceding companies of the same reinsurer, being involved in the same loss. However, an earthquake or hurricane can severely damage several metropolitan areas, causing heavy losses to all of the primary insurers actively writing business in those areas. As a result, the non-ocean marine excess reinsurer has to charge a loading which will yield a larger contribution to surplus than the ocean marine excess reinsurer.

The rate itself is expressed in terms of a percentage of the gross net premium income. This percentage is established by the excess underwriter determining what percentage of the estimated net premium income for the forthcoming year will yield the desired premium as obtained by the rating method.

There is one general factor which affects the rate of an excess of loss coverage left to be discussed and which will serve as the basis for another rating method. To recall, the general factors effecting the rate fall into four general categories: (1) the level of the net retention and the limit of liability of the reinsurer; (2) the range of business and whether the contract embodies the normal exclusions; (3) the past experience of the ceding company; and (4) the underwriting limits of the ceding company.

The underwriting limits of the ceding company in relation to the proposed net retention form the basis for the Exposure System of rating for an excess of loss contract. Under the exposure method, the rate is determined in relation to the reinsurer's direct exposure to the chance of loss in a method similar to the way the primary underwriter establishes his exposure. In addition to looking at the other factors previously mentioned, the reinsuring underwriter places a heavy emphasis on his direct exposure to a loss as the result of a loss occasioned by a single insured. For example, if the net retention were set at $50,000, and the amount retained net by the ceding company on the best class of risk were $100,000, the reinsurer would be directly exposed to the extent of $50,000. If a total loss were sustained by this class of risk, and the insurable value of the property were equal to the maximum underwriting limit, the excess reinsurer would be liable for $50,000 of the loss. Thus, the reinsuring underwriter could charge a rate which would be adequate for the risk assumed. Such an excess of loss contract would be called an exposed or "working" excess. The reinsurer may experience a loss under the contract as a result of a single insured incurring a heavy loss.

On the other hand, when the net reteniton is set at such a level that the ceding company's maximum commitment on any one risk does not reach or exceed the retention, the reinsurer is not directly exposed to the hazard insured by the ceding company. It cannot be interested in a loss by a single insured. A series of losses must be incurred in the same event before the reinsurer becomes involved. Thus, the reinsurer is unexposed to the original hazard and the cover has changed its character; it is now protecting the ceding company against another hazard, catastrophe. As a consequence, the excess underwriter cannot use the exposure method of rating.

When an excess of loss contract becomes unexposed, Burning Cost becomes the reinsuring underwriter's sole rating tool, even if it is a little crude, less refined, and totally un-actuarial. Sometimes, even the burning cost method must be given a little boost through some sort of "J" Factor thrown in by the underwriter. Circumstances which might give rise to such a "J" Factor are where there is a wide limit of liability, but little past experience; no losses exceeding the net retention in the last few years; or when there is some serious question about the "Incurred But Not Reported" reserves.

A word needs to be said concerning the desirability of the two rating methods in situations where either one may be used, i.e., on an exposed excess. Under the burning cost method, the rate is determined and renegotiated each year, reflecting the loss experience for the year just completed. Because of this readjustment, the costs of this coverage will increase as the loss experience gets progressively worse and the profit margins progressively smaller. When the insurer can least afford it, during the down side of the cycle, the cost of the coverage increases at a surprising rate. When the insurer can afford to pay a little more because of good experience, the cost of the coverage decreases. On the other hand, when the protection is rated on an exposure basis, the rate should remain the same year by year because the variations are supposedly included in the calculations of the rate. This avoids the difficulty of the protection costing more when the losses are heavy. Under the exposure method, the problem of maintaining a partial surplus for absorption of losses has been shifted from the company reinsured to the reinsurer. As a result, the reinsured loses the interest earned on the surplus passed to the reinsurer. The choice between the use of these two methods is the reinsurer's. There are times when one method is suprior to the other, and will vary from insurer to insurer, and within each insurer, from time to time.

System of Accounts

In contrast with the treaty system of accounts, the system used in excess of loss reinsurance is the utmost in simplicity and brevity. In excess of loss reinsurance, there are no monthly or quarterly accounts. The reinsured company pays an agreed amount at the first of the year; under certain circumstances, these payments may sometimes be quarterly. The rate itself may be of two types, (1) a set amount, such as $20,000 annually, or (2) a defined percentage of the estimated gross net premium income. The flat premium, as the set amount is called, is the normal method of charging the rate for pure catastrophe protection. The flat premium is charged rather than one which varies with the amount of earned premiums, because the reinsurers feel that the exposure to catastrophic losses is not going to vary much with a slow increase in the amount of business in force. Thus they charge a flat rate which may be adjusted every few years.

The second method of applying the rate for excess of loss coverage, as a percentage of the estimated gross net premium income, is used for all excess of loss reinsurances other than the pure catastrophe cover. The basis for this floating rate is that the exposure to loss varies in direct proportion to the amount of premiums earned. Under the floating rate, a minimum and deposit premium is required at the first of the year. The size of the minimum and deposit premium is dependent upon the estimated premium income for the ensuing year. It is normally set between 50 to 67 percent of the rate to be finally charged for the coverage. At the end of the year when the actual amount of the gross net premium income can be calculated, the full premium becomes due.

As an example of how the minimum and deposit premium works, suppose that the rate established through use of the burning cost formula is 5 percent of the annual gross net premium income. The GNPI has been estimated to be $500,000. The M & D Premium would be set at around 3 percent of the estimated GNPI, or $15,000, and would be payable shortly after the first of January. Assuming that the actual premium income equaled the estimated premium income, the remaining $10,000 would be due as soon after the end of the year as possible. If, on the other hand, the actual

GNPI is just $400,000, the ceding company would have to pay only an additional $5,000.

The premium paid by the ceding company is for a specific amount of protection, i.e., the reinsurer's limits of liability. A contract for $100,000 excess of $50,000, has the capacity to pay $100,000 in losses. Each loss paid under the contract reduces the available protection by that amount. In practice, however, the ceding company is seldom left with just this balance. The face of the contract is reinstated to the original amount, or $100,000 as in this example. This is normally on an automatic basis, the reinsurer automatically reinstating it to the original amount, and the ceding company automatically paying an additional premium as provided by the contract.

Depending upon the type of contract, the reinstatement may be automatic with or without an additional premium. In classes of business where the face amount of the original policy is not reduced because of loss, the standard practice is to automatically reinstate without additional premium. The reinstatement will require a pro-rata reinstatement premium in those classes of business where the original policy is reduced to correspond to any losses paid under the policy. The pro-rata payment provides that the reinsured pay for the additional coverage at the same rate, or in the same proportion, as it originally paid. Assume the reinsured company paid originally $5 per year per thousand dollars protection for an excess of loss contract. If a $50,000 loss occurred on the first day of the contract, the reinsured would be required to pay $250 for full reinstatement. If, on the other hand, the loss had occurred on the last day of the sixth month the contract was in force, the reinstatement premium would be $125 ($5 x 50 x ½ yr. = $125).

In addition to the reinstatement provision, the reinsurer limits the maximum aggregate amount of protection the contract may provide in any one year. The maximum aggregate amount is normally two or three times the face amount of the contract.

The following is an example of a reinstatement provision clause:

> In the event of loss or losses occurring hereunder, it is hereby mutually agreed to reinstate this reinsurance to its full amount of $100,000 from the time of the occurrence of such loss or losses to the expiry of this reinsurance. An additional premium calculated at pro-rata of $5,000 in full per annum for the period from the date of such loss or losses to expiry of this reinsurance shall be paid by the reinsured upon the amount of such loss or losses. This additional premium shall be paid by the reinsured when any loss or losses arising hereunder are settled. Not withstanding the foregoing, the reinsurer shall never be liable for more than $100,000 in respect of any one loss and/or occurrence, and not for more than $200,000 in all.

Loss Provisions

Since the year end statement of gross net premium income is the only report made to the reinsurers, there has to be some system of reporting and paying losses. Since excess of loss reinsurance is designed to place at the insurer's immediate disposal a large source of funds, the provisions for reporting and paying losses must allow this function to be realized. Generally, the reinsured is required to notify the reinsurer when it has reason to believe that a claim *will* exceed the net retention. The reinsurer is required to settle the claim thus submitted within fifteen to twenty days after receiving the notice of loss. The notice of loss needs to be only a well founded estimate. The reinsurers have to settle for the amount of estimated loss, and wait for an adjustment when the ultimate net loss is finally determined. A loss provision reads something like this:

> The reinsured company shall notify the reinsurers of any claim or claims advised to them which might give rise to a claim under this agreement as soon as the reinsured company has reason to believe that the reinsurers will be financially interested in such claim or claims. The reinsurer's proportion of such losses shall be payable within fifteen days of the receipt from the ceding company of the necessary papers proving the loss.

Criterion for Loss Assignment

As with treaty reinsurance, there must be a distinct method of determining what losses will come within the terms of the contract. Two such methods which predominate the usage at this time are (1) the losses incurred basis, and (2) the year of account basis. The objectives of the ceding company have to be considered when deciding which basis to use. If the purpose of the excess is to protect its treaty reinsurers for common account, the insurer will want to use the basis which best follows the treaty, i.e., the one which covers the treaty reinsurers as long as they are at risk. If the insurer is acquiring the excess to protect its own account, it would probably only be interested in the limits, or depth of coverage.

Under the losses occurring basis, all losses occurring within the period of the contract come within the scope of the contract, no matter under what underwriting year the original policy was issued. Thus, if a loss occurred on the tenth of January, it would come under the excess contract in effect at that time. The fact that the original policy was issued when there was another excess contract in force does not relieve the present reinsurer from liability. At the termination of the contract, the excess reinsurer ceases to be liable for any losses which occur after the contract expires. If a loss is in progress when the contract expires, the normal procedure is for the excess reinsurer under whose contract the commencement of the loss occurred to be liable for the entirety of the loss.

Because of the earned premium method of accounting in the United States, the losses-occurring basis is probably the predominate basis used in the non-ocean marine excess reinsurance area. In the earned premium basis in pro-rata reinsurance, the incoming treaty reinsurer assumes the risk portfolio from the outgoing reinsurer, thereby eliminating any run-off under the treaty. There is no problem of the excess contract written on a losses-occurring basis following the risks under the treaty. The excess is on a yearly basis and coincides with the treaty year basis of earned premiums, yielding no gap in excess coverage for the treaty reinsurers if the excess is for common account. If, however, the treaty which the losses occurring basis excess is protecting is on the policies attaching basis, the treaty reinsurers will be left uncovered at the end of the year should the excess is protecting is on the policies attaching basis, the treaty the policies attaching treaty. The primary insurer has warranted to its treaty reinsurers that they will be protected from excessive losses through "common account" reinsurance. As a result, the insurer runs the risk of acting as its own excess reinsurer for common account because it is not assured of continuous coverage of the treaty reinsurers.

In order to avoid the hazard of the excess reinsurer's cancelling and leaving the insurer having to protect the portfolio for the duration of the run-off, the year-of-account basis is used. This basis is also known under the name of the Treaty Year Basis and the Policies Attaching Basis. Under this basis, all losses are considered to be within the scope of the excess of loss contract so long as the policies under which they arise were issued during the period in which the excess contract was in effect. The excess reinsurer will be at risk until all of the risks ceded under the treaty for that year of account have expired and all losses settled. As a consequence, if the treaty has a long run-off, the excess contract will also have a long run-off. The advantage in the use of this basis is that the excess protection follows the treaty which it was purchased to protect. It may not be cancelled, leaving the ceding company exposed on the run-off. There are two primary disadvantages in the use of this basis, (1) the long run-off, and (2) the complications involved in keeping claims straight and assigning them to the proper excess reinsurer over a period of contract years.

The following is an example of a losses occurring provision and an associated clause.

> The reinsurers agree to reimburse the ceding company, on an excess of loss basis, for the amounts of ultimate net loss which the ceding company may pay or become liable to pay under its policies, as a result of any one loss or series of *losses* arising out of any one event, *occurring* on and after 12:01 P.M., Standard Time at the address of the insured of the ceding company's original policy . . .
>
> If this reinsurance should expire while a loss and/or occurrence and/or series of losses and/or occurrences arising out of one event is in progress, it is agreed that subject to the other conditions of this reinsurance, the reinsurers shall pay their proportion of the entire loss or damage, provided that the loss and/or occurrence and/or series of losses and/or occurrences arising out of the event commenced before the time of expiration of this contract.

FUNCTIONS OF EXCESS OF LOSS REINSURANCE

Excess of loss reinsurance is designed primarily to provide the insurer a way to protect itself against large losses which arise under the policies of insurance it issues. Excess of loss reinsurance enables the reinsured to definitely limit its amount of maximum possible loss to a level which its financial structure and premium volume can safely absorb. It also stabilizes the reinsured's loss ratio by allowing the heavy losses to be spread over a period of years. The spreading of losses over a period of years is accomplished through the rating system which allows the reinsurer to effectively "loan" the required sum needed by the reinsured at the time of loss.

The stabilizing effect excess reinsurance gives to the primary insurer is a protection it cannot obtain through the use of treaty reinsurance. The losses under treaty reinsurance are shared between the ceding company and the reinsurer, thereby not limiting the amount of variation, but simply reducing its intensity. It does not protect the insurer from an accumulation of losses. Down to a certain level of net retention, excess service is provided at less expense than treaty reinsurance. In addition, the administration required by excess reinsurance is truly the epitome of ease and simplicity.

There are certain disadvantages in the use of excess of loss reinsurance which should be considered. Because there is no actual cession of liability to the excess reinsurer as there is under treaty reinsurance, the reinsurer does not relieve the primary insurer of the responsibility of maintaining the unearned premium reserve for policies covered by the contract. As a consequence, the insurer has to pass up the growth financing which is available through the use of the other types of reinsurance, if excess is used exclusively. Another disadvantage in the use of excess of loss reinsurance arises as the net retention is lowered. Because the loading applied to the excess of loss rate is expressed as a percentage of the pure cost of the coverage, as the pure cost increases, the dollar amount of loading increases. As the net retention is progressively lowered, the larger the number of losses which exceed the net retention will become, the greater will be the pure cost, and the larger will be the dollar amount of loading. Soon the loading reaches a point where it increases astronomically unless some other method of rating is used, e.g., the exposure method.

A disadvantage to the reinsurer is the moral hazard to which the excess coverage is directly exposed. This is the moral hazard occasioned by the ceding company's underwriter who starts "writing against" the excess coverage. When writing against his excess of loss coverage, the underwriter does not maintain his previous underwriting standards. Contrary to the epitome of a virtuous primary underwriter, he ceases to underwrite as if he were completely exposed and not enjoying the protection afforded by the excess reinsurer. In setting the rate, the reinsuring underwriter had taken into consideration the primary insurer's underwriting policy. Any change in this policy nullifies, to a certain extent, the equity of the rate. On occasion, after the commencement of the excess contract, the primary underwriter increases the size or number of lines he will write on a risk. What was an unexposed excess coverage has become an exposed one, and claims occur which would never come under the contract as originally negotiated. Unfortunately, it is a natural tendency on the part of the primary underwriter to not forget that he has excess coverage, and precautions should be taken by both parties to limit this hazard to minor proportions.

EXCESS OF LOSS RATIO REINSURANCE

Another common form of excess reinsurance is excess of loss ratio reinsurance, or "stop-loss" reinsurance as it is sometimes called. Excess of loss ratio reinsurance is a reinsurance agreement under which the reinsurer is liable for any losses incurred by the ceding company on a particular line of business when the annual loss ratio exceeds an agreed percentage of its earned premium income for the line concerned. Under this form of excess reinsurance, the reinsurer is liable for all losses, no matter how small, which occur after an agreed loss ratio has been exceeded. The net retention is expressed as a specific loss ratio as are the reinsurer's limits. For example, the contract might provide that the reinsurer is liable for all losses in excess of a loss ratio of 65 percent up to and including a loss ratio of 120 percent. After the loss ratio exceeds 120 percent, the liability for any additional losses occurring during the year reverts back to the ceding company.

The reinsurer often requires the reinsured company to act as a co-reinsurer for a portion of the excess, thereby introducing some additional incentive for the primary insurer to maintain sound underwriting and claims policies. In such an instance, the limits might provide that the reinsurer is only liable for 80 percent of all losses in excess of a loss ratio of 65 percent up to and including a loss ratio of 120 percent. The reinsured is required to act as its own co-reinsurer for the balance, 20 percent. In referring to the co-reinsurance practice, C.E. Golding said:

> It is a well established reinsurance principle that it is not wise, except in very special circumstances, to accept liability for the whole of a claim or series of claims, the settlement of which is left entirely in the hands of the ceding company. Such a condition of affairs, without any reflection whatever on the honesty of the ceding company, is likely to lead to some relaxation on the methods of claim settlements to the prejudice of the reinsurer.[3]

An essential consideration in establishing the net retention is the insurer's average expense ratio. The net retention must be set at a level which does not guarantee a profit to the ceding company. It must be set so that there is little, if any, margin between the level of the retention plus the expense ratio and one hundred percent.

Excess of loss ratio reinsurance is designed to protect the primary insurers from loss due to an aggregation of small losses. This protection is the advantage, under certain circumstances, in the use of the excess of loss ratio form of excess over the straight excess of loss form. In certain classes of business, the vast majority of claims are limited to relatively small amounts, e.g., automobile property damage. In these classes, the use of excess of loss with its accompanying dollar level of net retention would require the net retention being set so low that the cost would be unreasonable. However, the primary insurer needs some form of excess reinsurance to ensure that the aggregate value of these small claims do not exceed the premium income for the class. The excess of loss ratio form satisfies this need nicely.

[3] C. E. Golding, *The Law and Practice of Reinsurance*. (London: Buckley Press Ltd., 1954.); p. 133.

In classes of business where there might be some difficulty in accurately establishing whether the losses were due to one or more causes, the excess of loss ratio reinsurance is superior to excess of loss. The former does not require that "any one event" be defined. Its only concern is that the loss can be established as being within a specific year. Crop hail is such a class which frequently presents the problem of determining "any one event." It is difficult for either party to prove whether the hail losses in a brief period of days were due to one or many hail storms. Excess of loss ratio reinsurance is often valuable in providing meaningful reinsurance in this area.

There are two distinct disadvantages to the use of excess of loss ratio reinsurance. First, the reinsurer does not furnish cash when the ceding company needs it in order to settle heavy losses. Settlements under the contract are made after the end of the year when sufficient information is available to establish reasonably accurate losses incurred and earned premiums for the year. Not withstanding the settlement provision, the reinsurer *may* advance some money if the retention clearly has been exceeded during the year. This practice eases the intensity of this disadvantage, but does not overcome it.

The second disadvantage in the use of the excess of loss ratio reinsurance is the co-reinsurer provision requiring a 20 percent participation by the reinsured company. The reinsured company is not able to definitely limit its losses. It does a better job of this in certain classes, however, than the excess of loss form that does not act directly on loss ratio. While these two disadvantages are not severe, the insurer who chooses to utilize this form of excess protection must do so with care. It should particularly ensure that its cash flow is large enough to allow it to not require immediate cash in the event of a serious run of losses.

SPECIAL FORMS OF EXCESS REINSURANCE

Often an insurer finds that its needs are not completely satisfied with the more or less standard forms of excess reinsurance. It thus becomes the responsibility of some ingenious person on the reinsurer's staff to set up a special plan which will satisfy the needs of the insurer and yet be acceptable to the reinsurer. A plan can be created which can satisfy any needs, no matter how ridiculous or far fetched. However, once such a plan has been drawn up, some reinsurer must be convinced that it is in its best interests as well as the insurer's to assume liability under the plan. Such a task is not an easy one, e.g., one case in point, a forethinking chief executive spent approximately two years developing an adequate plan for his company. He then had to devote another year of hard selling here and in London before it could actually be put into effect.

The Carpenter Plan

The Carpenter Plan is a method of excess reinsuring whereby the reinsurer agrees to reimburse the reinsured company for all losses, or a large portion thereof, in excess of a schedule of net retentions which vary according to the type of risk reinsured. It is the practice with this form of excess for the reinsurer's limits of liability to vary with the level of the net retention in a manner similar to the surplus reinsurer's which also varies with the amount of liability retained by the ceding company. For example, the operative clause of the contract will include a table of limits similar to the following:

CLASS OF RISK	REINSURER'S LIABILITY	NET RETENTION
A	$100,000 in excess of	$12,000
B	75,000 in excess of	10,000
C	50,000 in excess of	7,000
D	40,000 in excess of	5,000

This series of net retentions strongly resembles the surplus treaty, the retentions being greater for the best class of risks (Class A) and less significant for the less desirable classes. The varying of the net retentions is an effort to extract some of the rigidity inherent in the standard excess of loss contract, thereby yielding it capable of imparting a degree of homogeneity to the reinsured's portfolio, as is the with the use of the surplus treaty.

The reinsurer's limits of liability vary because of the selection against the reinsurer which is built into a system allowing the insurer to retain smaller limits on poor risks than on good ones. To a degree, the reinsurer is able to offset this selection by reducing the amount of its liability on the poorer risks. If the reinsurance agreement so developed can effectively replace the insurer's surplus treaty, the insurer will reduce both the reinsurance administration costs and the amount of premium income passed on to the reinsurer.

The rate for the Carpenter Plan is expressed as a percentage of the reinsured's premium income in the same manner as the standard excess of loss contract. The normal rating system is that of burning cost plus a loading of 100/60 to 100/75; however, the pure cost is more difficult to obtain. In order to establish an accurate loss picture under the Carpenter Plan, the reinsurer must not only determine the losses which exceeded the net retention in the last five years, but also group them into the classes of risk from which they emanated. In the event two insureds are involved in the same loss, both being from different classes, the normal procedure is for the loss retention of the best class involved in the loss to be the net retention and reinsurer's limit of liability applied.

The Carpenter Plan imparts a good deal of flexibility to the excess of loss cover; however, since it is fundamentally designed to replace an underlying surplus treaty, certain disadvantages arise. First, the insurer does not find any relief from its reinsurance program on losses of a moderate nature. If, for some reason, these small losses happened to increase in number, they could severely distort the loss ratio, thereby reducing the value of the protection afforded by the excess. If, on the other hand, a surplus treaty were being used, these losses would be shared proportionately between the ceding company and the reinsurer. The ceding company would have reinsurance protection which a series of losses would find more difficult to seriously affect the loss ratio. Secondly, if the excess is to impart size homogeneity to the portfolio, the net retentions have to be so low that the cover can become rather costly. The cost disadvantage would hold true unless some system other than burning cost is used as the rating base. In recognition of the high cost, primary insurers who utilize the Carpenter Plan normally sacrifice a degree of homogeneity by placing the net retentions slightly higher than they would be if a surplus treaty were used. The net retentions are set just high enough to attain a significant reduction in the cost of the protection.[4]

Excess of Average Loss Reinsurance

The excess of average loss form of excess reinsurance is sometimes used by a primary insurer to protect a small fire account. Basically it is an excess of loss ratio type contract, the retention being set at the average loss ratio for the last ten years. It is common for the reinsurer to participate in approximately twenty-five percent of the losses which do not exceed the loss ratio, and to assume liability for around seventy-five percent of the losses in excess of the net retention. The excess of average loss form is rated at burning cost as determined from the losses over the last ten years. A loading varying from fifteen to twenty-five percent is also applied.

[4]See Table VI, "A Comparison of Relative Costs of A 'Working' Excess of Loss Contract At Varying Limits of Net Retention," page 107 for a tabular display of this effect.

Excess of average loss is a very simple form of excess coverage, requiring little labor other than that required for preparation of the annual statements. Because of its heavy participation as a co-reinsurer, the insurer using this form of excess should have a relatively small account where the very maximum possible loss due to a catastrophe or series of catastrophes could not aggregate sufficient losses to jeopardize its overall annual loss ratio.

Aggregating Excess of Loss

The aggregating excess of loss contract is growing in popularity among insurers as a form of catastrophe protection in the property lines. Its popularity is due to the recognition by reinsurance buyers that they want to protect their annual loss ratio first and their surplus secondly. The standard catastrophe excess takes the form of a high net retention excess of loss, the net retention being anywhere from one-half of one percent to two percent, or more, of the annual premiums written. This effectively protests the insurer from a single catastrophe increasing its over all loss ratio more than the one or two percent. However, what happens when more than one catastrophe occurs during the year? The standard catastrophe protection does not do the job.

The aggregating excess is designed to solve the problem of accumulation of catastrophies. In order to do this, two net retentions are established, a lower one set at a level over which a few losses occur during the year, and an upper net retention set at a level generally one to two percent of the insurer's annual premiums written. In order for the reinsured to collect from the reinsurer, the *aggregate* losses during the year *in excess* of the lower net retention must exceed the upper net retention. The reinsurer then pays all losses in excess of the lower net retention for the remainder of the year. This protects the insurer's overall annual loss ratio from being effected more than one or two percentage points by catastrophies or heavy losses in any one year.

An aggregating excess can be particularly useful to insurers writing in the Midwest, or "Tornado Belt," where generally the wind losses do not reach the proportions of the coastal storms, but are more frequent. The following Table demonstrates the advantage of the aggregating excess over the normal catastrophe excess of loss to such an insurer.

Assume the insurer's premiums written are around $200,000,000. The net retention for both excesses was set at one percent, yet the high retention excess allowed the catastrophics/losses in one year to increase the loss ratio by 3.45 percent. The aggregating excess allowed an increase of 1.9 percent in the loss ratio. When most profit margins are in terms of one percent or less, the protection afforded by the aggregating excess can be quite important.

Generally the aggregating excess will be "working" more than the high net retention excess, and thus will have a higher rate. The rate is calculated by the burning cost method using the last five years' loss experience and is expressed as a percentage of premiums earned. By using an aggregating excess and letting it work, the insurer is substituting a slow fluctuation in expense for a more volitile fluctuation in loss ratio.

AGGREGATING EXCESS AND THE HIGH RETENTION CATASTROPHE EXCESS OF LOSS RECOVERIES COMPARED

CATASTROPHE/LOSS	NET LOSS TOTAL	EXCESS RECOVERY[1] HIGH RETENTION	EXCESS RECOVERY[2] AGGREGATING
Tornado	$ 450,000	$ 0	$ 0
Tornado	600,000	0	0
Industrial-Fire	$ 550,000	0	0
Tornado	700,000	0	0
Industrial-Fire	350,000	0	0
Tornado	650,000	0	100,000
Hurricane	1,200,000	0	1,000,000
Industrial-Fire	400,000	0	200,000
Hurricane	3,100,000	1,100,000	2,900,000
TOTAL	$8,000,000	$1,100,000	$4,200,000

[1]Net Retention $2,000,000
[2]Net Retention $2,000,000 aggregate of excess losses in excess of $200,000

The Umbrella Coverage

The "Umbrella" is the name given to a colossal excess of loss contract, or series of contracts, which protects the insurer's entire portfolio to the exclusion of any other form or type of reinsurance. This is the characteristic from whence it derives its name. It is the insurer's sole protection in the form of a single contract, or single type of contract, giving total reinsurance coverage. This is simply the standard excess of loss contract which in its operative clause, instead of including within the scope of the contract one or two lines of business, includes all of the various classes of insurance written by ing classes of business: fire and allied lines, marine, inland marine, the insurer. For example, one particular umbrella covers the follow- miscellaneous casualty, workman's compensation, general liability, and automobile third party liability. All of these lines are covered for both domestic and foreign business.

Because of the large range of liability and the necessity of high limits of liability, it is difficult for such a coverage to be placed in a single market. The magnitude of this problem can be appreciated when one considers that the reinsuring underwriters who participate, or who are approached for participation, are in the business of assuming liability under reinsurances which cover only one or a few lines of business. Their underwriting policies are constructed to allow for profitable operation in this manner. As a consequence, the underwriter has to justify a deviaiton from the underwriting policies to both his superiors and his retrocessionaires. Further, because of the large limits of liability on the total coverage, the market may become saturated, leaving a portion of the contract unassumed. In order to alleviate this problem, the coverage is invariably split into several layers. Thus, the various reinsurers are able to assume small shares of liability in selected layers to suit their underwriting policies and judgment. The umbrella previously referred to is composed of six layers as follows: $425,000 excess of $75,000; $3,000,000 excess of $500,000; $3,000,000 excess of $3,500,000; $3,500 000 excess of $6,500,000; and $10,000,000 excess of $10,000,000.

The advantages in the use of the umbrella coverage are two-fold. First, it is the epitome of simplicity, requiring little effort and administrative expense; and secondly, the amount of premium income passed to the reinsurer's coffers is considerably reduced. Although these are substantial advantages, the insurer who considers shifting to this form of reinsurance program should be aware of the limitations. Because of its uniform net retention applying over the whole portfolio, it is not sufficiently flexible to meet the need for grading the retention according to the class or quality of risk in order to enhance profitability. There is no protection from moderate sized losses. Further, assuming that it would be replaicng some treaties, the company would presumably reduce its overhead expenses previously associated with the handling of reinsurance by transferring the reinsurance staff to other duties. After a period of years, if the company finds that the umbrella is not satisfactory, it would be difficult to rebuild the necessary organization for a return to the use of automatic pro-rata reinsurance.

CHAPTER SUMMARY

Excess reinsurance may be defined as reinsurance agreements whereby the reinsurer agrees to reimburse the reinsured company for all losses, or a large portion thereof, over a certain relatively high limit (net retention), for consideration of a percentage of the reinsured company's net premiun income. Under this type of reinsurance agreement, the reinsurer does not share in all losses, as do treaty reinsurers. The reinsurer is not interested in a loss until it exceeds the net retention. The reinsurer is solely liable for the excess loss.

Excess reinsurance differs from automatic pro-rata (Treaty) reinsurance in the following manner. (1) The treaty is a sharing agreement between the ceding company and the reinsurer. In excess reinsurance, the parties remain individually liable. (2) The rate charged by the treaty reinsurer is the original premium paid by the insured less a commission. The rate charged by the excess reinsurer is calculated independently of the reinsured company's rates charged for the original coverage. (3) Treaty settlements are made at the end of each reporting period, monthly or quarterly, by account. Excess settlements are by cash when the loss is determined. (4) The primary insurer is the insured. There are primarily two methods of actually calculating the rate for excess reinsurance, burning cost and exposure. Burning cost is basically past experience, whereas the exposure basis is an actuarially calculated rate based upon exposure to chance of loss.

The excess premium is due at the commencement of the cover, and normally yearly thereafter. Claims which arise under the contract are reported as soon as possible to the reinsurer who then must settle the claim within a relatively short period of time, normally fifteen to twenty days. The characteristics outlined above impart to excess of loss reinsurance the ability to protect the primary insurer against excessive losses and to stabilize its loss ratio. It does not, however, protect the insurer against the ravages of a multitude of moderate losses, nor does it relieve the insurer from its burden of maintaining the unearned premium reserve.

Excess of loss ratio reinsurance is designed to protect primary insurers subject to only the mildest of shock losses. Their portfolio is characterized by the number of small or moderate losses which arise thereunder. In excess of loss ratio reinsurance, the reinsured company's net retention is set at a specific annual loss ratio. Once the loss ratio is exceeded in any one year, the reinsurer assumes a large portion of the excess losses (normally between 80 to 90 percent). Although this protects the ceding company against a deluge of moderate losses, its relief is limited in a major catastrophe. As a consequence, the primary insurer who utilizes excess of loss ratio reinsurance must be assured of a source of temporary funds in the event a heavy loss is experienced.

Part II

Buying Reinsurance

The buyer of reinsurance faces the problem of deciding what reinsurance to buy and how much. This is not an easy task. If done properly, a systematic approach must be followed in applying certain well defined principles. Part II consists of three chapters designed to assist the reinsurance buyer in this evolution. One chapter is devoted to the actual development of a reinsurance program. The selection of a reinsurer and a broker is considered in the next chapter, and the final chapter takes an indepth look at the practice of reciprocity.

CHAPTER V

Reinsurance Programming

THIS CHAPTER is devoted to developing a logical method of establishing an optimum reinsurance program. There are few hard-and-fast rules to guide the executive in his efforts in establishing a program of reinsurance; however, one bit of good advice would be to follow a definite path or set series of considerations each time the program is considered. The object of following a distinct path in establishing a reinsurance program is to give the insurer a better-than-even chance of establishing a reinsurance program which will conform to the insurer's individual requirements as closely as the Market will allow. The "path" to the optimal program must begin with an investigation of underwriting policies and the reinsurance support they require. The next phase is the matching of reinsurance coverages to these underwriting needs (market and cost considerations will always require some compromise). The final phase is the planning and placement of the catastrophe program.

The guiding principle throughout the programming technique is that a change in the foundation of the program – underwriting policy and philosophy – will probably effect the entire structure. The executive must continually be aware of this principle and alter the program as the underwriting policy changes. If this is not done, soon a program of reinsurance will exist which does not match needs. As a result, losses will occur which are not properly covered and scarce expense dollars are wasted.

Appendix B, "The Programming Sequence, Statistics, and Exhibits," contains a flow chart displaying the various phases involved in the logical development of a reinsurance program. Its purpose is to act as a guide to persons carrying out the programming task. Included in this appendix is a list of the statistics by major line required in order to enable an adequate program to be developed. The reinsurance analyst can duplicate this list and give it to each department head concerned, thereby facilitating his efforts. Finally, a list of the normal programming exhibits is included in Appendix B along with example exhibits. These are the exhibits the writer has found most helpful in setting up the final program and in selling it to management. Variations of these four basic exhibits should satisfy most of the needs of the analyst. By including these examples as a standardizing technique, none of the intrigue in programming has been eliminated. The numerous special situations that exist within each company will always require the analyst to utilize some ingenuity in displaying a situation in such a manner as to allow it to be easily analyzed.

DETERMINATION OF GENERAL NEEDS

The first general area of consideration is determining what reinsurance support needs are required by underwriting; and what type of reinsurance agreement is best suited for satisfying those needs. The various objectives of reinsurance have been discussed in the preceding chapters in considerable detail. A re-grouping and summation of the various objectives is required, the purpose being to set out which types of reinsurance agreements perform each function and how well they do so.

To Stabilize Annual Loss Experience

A relatively stable loss ratio is the mark of a sound insurer. To the inquiring individual, stable annual results indicates certain aspects of a sound reinsurance program as well as sound underwriting policies. No matter who the inquirer is – insurer, examiner, salesman, or prospect – a stable loss ratio is an indication of a well managed company. As a result, the stabilizing function of reinsurance has received, and probably always will receive, careful attention and top priority on the part of the insurer.

When properly arranged, the excess forms of reinsurance can contribute a great deal toward the stabilization of loss experience. Unless the insurer's underwriting policies are basically sound, a stable loss ratio is an impossibility, no matter how well planned and organized the reinsurance program. If, for some reason, an error in underwriting judgment is made, a good reinsurance program will give the insurer time to correct its mistake without too great a fluctuation in experience.

Excess of Loss Ratio is designed to stabilize the loss ratio. It assumes a large portion, ninety percent for example, of all settlements in excess of a loss ratio of a certain percentage. Excess of loss, however, accomplishes its stabilizing effect in two ways. First, it definitely limits the amount of possible loss in any one event under all but abnormal circumstances. By setting the proper retention on the excess of loss through bringing into harmony the frequency and size of losses, the insurer can achieve relative stability. Secondly, by virtue of the rating method most commonly used in the lower levels of "working" excess (Burning Cost), the excess losses of the primary insurer are spread over a period of years. This is why excess of loss reinsurance, when so rated, is often called "Spread Loss." The rate is simply the average amount of excess losses over the net retention during the rating period (normally five years) plus the loading. In this way, the ceding company effectively pays the reinsurer for its "loan" over the rating period. The insurer substitutes small fluctuations in expense ratio for larger fluctuations in loss ratio.

To Protect Surplus

The function of an insurer's surplus is often stated to be that of absorbing any large losses or series of losses which, without surplus, would seriously jeopardize the financial well-being of the insurer. However, most executives will state that while this may be the use to which surplus is applied during heavy loss periods, it is to reinsurance that this burden falls under normal circumstances. While all of the basic forms of reinsurance protect surplus to a certain degree, the bulwark between the impact of heavy losses and the insurer's surplus is normally excess reinsurance, either Excess of Loss or Excess of Loss Ratio.

In excess of loss reinsurance, the reinsurer steps into the picture when a relatively large loss has been sustained. It is best suited, therefore, as a protection of surplus for the classes of direct business which have characteristics of (1) wide fluctuations in loss experience with the largest losses being relatively substantial, or (2) being subject to catastrophic losses. An example of a class of business in which excess of loss is particularly valuable is the private passenger auto policy. The majority of the third party claims are less than $5,000, but losses of relatively high amounts do occur. The homeowner's class is also extremely vulnerable to catastrophe losses, not only through conflagaration but also from windstorm and hail damage under the extended coverage portion of the policy.

While excess of loss reinsurance might meet the requirements of many classes of business, insurers have found that in certain cases, excess of loss ratio has a greater appeal. The normal area in which this form is preferred is that class of business in which (1) the characteristic loss is one of rather small dimensions, (2) there is a great chance that the volume of these small losses may absorb too much of the premium income, and (3) there is a large fluctuation in the loss ratio from year to year. A good example of this is in the physical damage section of the automobile policy where the size of individual losses are small in comparison to the other insurance coverages, but collectively have the habit of running through the year's premium income with embarrassing regularity. Further, the catastrophe hazard in this class of business is relatively negligible.

While it is easily seen that excess of loss is not needed to protect surplus in the automobile collision risk, the disadvantages in the use of excess of loss ratio to protect surplus in other classes such as the homeowner's policy is not so apparent. There is one dividing characteristic of the two forms which indicates which form is more appropriate — that of time of payment. Speed in payment is an essential characteristic of excess of loss reinsurance. It is designed to act as a reserve account upon which the reinsured can draw when a large loss occurs.

In contrast, the excess of loss ratio reinsurer only settles the account well after the end of the year, unless otherwise agreed, when all of the loss figures are in and an accurate estimation of outstanding losses can be made. Thus, an insurer who uses excess of loss ratio where excess of loss should be used will find that (1) periodically a group of investments will have to be quickly liquidated and (2) a large cash reserve has to be maintained in order to meet claims as they arise. If excess of loss were used, these reserves probably could be converted into profitable, long term investments and periodic panics avoided.

To Reduce the Conflagration Hazard

Although in certain areas of property insurance catastrophes and conflagrations are bound to occur, it is the goal of every underwriter to successfully limit his losses in a catastrophe to relatively minor proportions.[1] In classes where a definite figure can be obtained as to the insurer's commitment in specified areas, such as used to be obtained in fire insurance through an accurate indexing system, the exposure to the effects of a conflagration can be effectively reduced by use of pro-rata reinsurance (facultative or treaty reinsurance). By this method, the underwriter can prudently lower aggregate commit-

[1]A reader of the manuscript stated that a good fire or marine underwriter would be perturbed if a large factory burned or a large vessel were lost, and he did not participate. It would indicate that something is wrong with his spread.

ments in an area and isolate risks by systematically reinsuring certain ones.

The pro-rata method is fine when the subject matter of insurance is stationary and of a relatively certain value, but the underwriter who has insured risks which have the quality of mobility finds incomplete relief in pro-rata reinsurance due to possible accumulation of risk. The underwriter whose insureds remain relatively stationary but whose hazards are mobile, such as windstorms, finds more relief from the pro-rata reinsurer but not enough to consider it complete protection. Underwriters in both cases, being unable to reduce the hazard to a comfortable level, utilize excess of loss to protect against the unexpected and unavoidable accumulation of risks.

To Yield Homogeneity

It is a well recognized fact that in order for the Law of Large Numbers to operate effectively, homogeneity of risk must be attained. The closer the homogeneity, the closer the results obtained will approach the results expected. The underwriter is able to classify risks by quality and rate them accordingly. Unless the variation in size of the individual risks is relatively narrow in each class, the loss experience will still vary widely from expected experience. The reason is, of course, that homogeneity must be accomplished both in quality and size.

For the large insurer who has a sizable volume of business and a wide spread, variations from the average risk per class will be relatively minor, assuming there are enough classes. Homogeneity in such cases can be considered obtained, for the variations in size will have a negligible effect on the results. Any glaring variations, however, should be reduced by use of facultative reinsurance, thereby reducing the chance of wide variation in experience.

The insurer who does not have a wide spread and large volume of business cannot effectively operate and ignore relatively strict size homogeneity. The variations from the average size of risks per class will be of such magnitude that facultative placements become impractical. The Surplus Treaty was developed to give the insurer size homogeneity in such cases. It effectively limits the ceding company's retained line to manageable limits and allows it to balance both the size and the quality of risks accepted.

The Carpenter Plan was developed because of the relative cost of administering a surplus treaty as compared to quota share and excess reinsurance. The purpose of this plan was to approach size homogeneity from another angle, that is, from the variation in losses from the average losses per class instead of variation in exposure. By reporting only claims in excess of the underlying retention, the administration costs can be reduced considerably from that of the surplus treaty. Homogeneity is attained, to a certain degree, by the variation in retention between classes. In order to keep the rate for this cover at a reasonable level, the net retention has to be set at a higher level than most smaller insurers require for the purpose of establishing homogeneity. Such a high schedule of net retentions often off-sets the advantages the Carpenter Plan might otherwise offer.

For Surplus Relief

To the smaller insurer striving to expand premium income as rapidly as possible, the strain on its relatively limited surplus is a definite limiting factor on the rate of growth. This limitation comes about because of the unearned premium reserve requirement. The conflict of having to place all of its premium income in a reserve account, and yet pay the agent's commission and associated costs of putting the business on the books, puts the insurer in a difficult position. These expenses are paid out of surplus until some of the unearned premium reserve is earned. It is thus easy to see that this reserve requirement, ignoring reinsurance for the moment, definitely limits the rate of expansion an insurer may attain.

Fortunately, when an insurer passes on a portion of its liability to a reinsurer, it is relieved of having to maintain that portion of the unearned premium reserve on the liability ceded.[2] The reinsurance commission given to the ceding company for the cession can then be used to meet its expenses, thereby reducing the drain on surplus for this purpose. The reinsurer thus plays a valuable role in the growth and development of the industry. Without this financing, the market capacity would be far from what it is today.

The forms of reinsurance which allow this financing are prorata facultative and treaty reinsurances. Excess reinsurance does not possess this attribute, as it is reinsurance of losses, not risks. One of the primary differences between excess reinsurance and the other forms is that in excess reinsurance, individual risks are not shared with the reinsurer in any predetermined proportions; therefore, the reinsurer cannot assume any unearned premium reserve on these risks.

To Eenter a New Geographical Area or Class of Business

When a primary insurer enters into a new area or class of busi-

[2]In certain states, unless a reinsurer is licensed to do business therein, the primary insurer is not relieved of the responsibility of maintaining the unearned premium reserve. In such instances the reinsurer is said to be "non-admitted."

ness, it is definitely limited as to the form of reinsurance it may use. Certain forms of reinsurance which may be acceptable to the insurer are unacceptable to a reinsurer. The problem of the conflict of interest between the two parties arises because of the initially small number of policies in force. The lack of sufficient volume to allow the Law of Large Numbers to operate efficiently, normally results in a wide variation of actual from expected loss experience.

The primary insurer would prefer to use a surplus treaty which gives it, on an automatic basis, both size homogeneity and a larger share of the good risks and a small share of the bad ones. As a result, the insurer can come closer to showing a profitable entry. The reinsurer, realizing he will be bearing a disproportionate part of the load, may be willing only to offer the primary insurer either a quota share treaty or, in certain instances, excess of loss coverage. The problem with the excess of loss, and the reason it is seldom used at this stage, is that there is no past experience upon which to base the rate. It is extremely difficult to establish a rate which is equally fair to both parties. The new account will be so unbalanced that the reinsurer will require too high a proportion of the premium.

Quota share reinsurance, then, is the form of reinsurance normally agreed upon by both parties for use when the primary insurer is entering a new area or class of business. In order to compensate for not having reinsurance facilities to furnish automatic size homogeneity, the primary insurer is forced to select risks carefully, both by size and by quality. The reinsurer is assured of getting a fair share of every risk written, no matter what the size or quality. It will thus share the fortunes of the ceding company identically.

To Withdraw From An Area or Class of Business

In order to brace up its underwriting policies or correct a bad swing in experience, an insurer sometimes is faced with the necessity of consolidating its writings and withdrawing from the area or class concerned. In the withdrawal situation, there are basically two approaches that may be used by the insurer for handling the business that is on the books. The first of these is for service branches to be maintained in the area and the existing policies "run-off" to termination. This is, of course, a long process. There is a danger that bad experience will continue to be reflected in the loss ratio for the duration of the run-off, with costs aggrevated by the expense of maintaining a service organization or paying for an independent adjustor.

The second method of withdrawal is that of selling the entire book of business to another insurer. This transaction is commonly called portfolio reinsurance. The entire liability is ceded to the reinsurer, and new policies normally are not issued to the policyholder until expiration of the ceded policy. Legally, however, this form of transaction is more accurately called "substitution," for the reinsurer is directly liable to the insured.[3] The true form of portfolio reinsurance is better illustrated in treaty transfers. All of the risks that are outstanding when the treaty is cancelled are assumed by another reinsurer, the ceding company still retaining a portion of the liability.

To Protect Treaty Reinsurers

The desirability of any business venture is directly related to the amount of profit expected to be gained from participation in the activity. Recognizing this fact, certain primary insurers developed methods designed to keep their treaties on a profitable basis. In this way, they maintain a good bargaining position, a wealth of prospective reinsurers, and the best rates the Market has to offer. Basically, of course, the profit to be made is a function of the ceding company's underwriting policy; however, as business runs in cycles, so does loss experience, and what is a profitable treaty today may not be so desirable five years from now. The long term trends in the cycle cannot be avoided, but a treaty can be protected from the effects of occasional poor underwriting judgment or bad luck if the ceding company exercises a little caution and forethought.

The occasional risks of a questionable nature which are accepted by the ceding company probably should be reinsured outside the treaty through facultative cessions in order to protect the treaty. A judicious sprinkling of this sort of thing goes a surprisingly long way in maintaining the treaty's profitability.

Another method of protecting the treaty from a shock loss standpoint is through the use of excess of loss reinsurance for the benefit of the treaty reinsurers. This is called reinsurance for "common account." By reinsuring for common account, the ceding company arranges for excess of loss reinsurance to protect the risks ceded under the treaty against the effects of a catastrophe. Since common account reinsurance is paid for by the treaty reinsurers, it must be determined which reinsurer wants the protection and which does not. Those who indicate their desire for the protection, pay a prorata proportion of the cost of the cover and receive the benefit of their share in any recoveries under the excess of loss reinsurance. Those reinsurers who decline the cover may do so because they are able to absorb major losses incurred from the treaty concerned under their own excess of loss contracts.

[3]See *Sachs v. Ohio National Life Insurance Company*, 322 U.S. 706.

To Support Group Member

Seldom, if ever, are all members of a newly organized group of companies of such financial strength that one or more could not use a little support from its group members. A method of providing this support is through an exchange of reinsurance treaties between the weak member and the rest of the group. This is accomplished by the weak member setting up a surplus treaty that has retentions set in such a manner that the large portion of the losses are passed on to its reinsurers (group members). It retains a large portion of the low hazard risks and retains little of the high hazard ones. In all probability, the weak member will show nice profits, and the stronger members will make little, if any, profit on the treaty.[4]

To Spread Risk

In an effort to achieve even a greater spread of risk than they can get through their direct writings, many insurers divide their treaties up into small shares, giving each share to a different reinsurer in return for a small share of their treaty. This concept of reciprocity effectively increases the insurer's base upon which the law of averages will work. As a result, the annual results will become more predictable. The pro-rata treaties are the normal vehicles for such an exchange, although the costs of administration must be carefully watched lest they get out of hand.

Class or Blanket Reinsurance

Ever present in determining an insurer's general reinsurance needs and how these needs are best met, is the conflict between the proponents of "class" reinsurance and the proponents of blanket, or "company" reinsurance. The proponents of class reinsurance have as their basic premise that they are better able to assume exactly the risks they are in businses to assume; that they have a greater control over the liability assumed and ceded; and, finally, that they know exactly where they stand in each class of business written, and not just a vague idea. The proponents of blanket reinsurance believe

[4]It is recognized that this section "has nothing to do with Pukka Reinsurance," to quote a manuscript reader. However, this use of reinsurance is presented as it is used, as an alternative to direct financial support of a group member. Although this is not "true" reinsurance in that the concept presented herein is contrary to sound reinsurance theory and practice, a discussion of the uses to which reinsurance can be applied would be incomplete without it. Before utilizing reinsurance in this way, the responsible executives should ensure that they are in no way acting in other than the best interests of their stockholders by passing profits on to another company in this manner.

that, to the greatest extent possible, an insurer's program should be geared to the overall performance of the company, with the minimum attention being paid to the individual classes. Supporting their contention is the industry-wide trend toward package policies and a growing concept of account underwriting instead of individual risk underwriting. Packages and account underwriting are placing a greater and greater pressure on the primary insurer to use blanket coverage in its reinsurance program. On the other hand, there exists an incompatability of different lines for reinsurance purposes because of loss lag (property, 45 days; liability, several years; workman's compensation, decades) which must be recognized.[5]

Some of the answers to this conflict may lie in the recognition of the varying validity of the respective arguments. There are certain circumstances which suggest that one form is more in accordance with the overall objectives of management than the other. Generally, the criterion upon which the choice has been made by many insurers runs as follows. Blanket coverage is normally sound when the line of business being reinsured has the following characteristics. (1) The circumstances likely to give rise to a claim vary widely. (2) Hazardous risks possess not only a greater chance of loss but also a much greater potential cost. The risk presents a relatively unknown factor as to the exact chance of loss and possesses a large loss potential. A good example of a general area of hazards that possesses the above characteristics is that of third party liability where the best insured may present the heaviest loss. Because of the impossibility of determining "quality" of risks, the results are unpredictable and, therefore, more suited to blanket protection through an excess contract than through class coverage. Class coverage is normally best used when the class of business being reinsured has the following characteristics. (1) Frequency rather than severity of the individual claims is affected. (2) The size of possible loss can be accurately evaluated. An example of a general area of hazards which possesses the above named characterisitics is that of property damage, here the retention can be individually set so as to handle the "known" risk and yield homogeneity.

When deciding whether to utilize class or blanket coverage, a characteristic of the class coverage should be considered. If class coverage is predominantely used, there is a great danger of "over-reinsurance." Henry Kramer put this point very nicely when he said, "As a geneal observation, however, I believe that a very great danger of reinsurance is over reinsurance, and a sure way to get there is to

[5]For a detailed discussion of the package problem, see "Packages," page 100.

follow a class reinsurance program. You may have happy contented underwriters if you do it, but others, such as stockholders, may wonder why the wheels are running down.[6]

PRESENT REINSURANCE PRACTICES

An analysis of the general reinsurance needs of an insurer reveals definite areas or objectives to which a reinsurance program must be tailored. A recognition of what forms of reinsurance are generally best suited to meet these needs is of vital importance. Of equal importance is the understanding of just how insurers are actually utilizing their reinsurance facilities. In this section, an attempt has been made to isolate the major classes of insurance and to present the types of reinsurance generally used by insurers engaged in the acceptance of insurance in those classes.

Fire and Property Damage

The most common arrangement in the fire and property damage class is a surplus or quota share treaty for the area of exposure per individual risk, with catastrophe protection in the form of an excess of loss contract. The tendency is to use a surplus treaty, if possible, in order to attain size homogeneity and to limit the commitment on any one risk to manageable proportions. The underlying retention for the excess of loss contract is then set at the maximum underwriting limit, or some other applicable high figure, which limits the claims that fall within the terms of the excess contract to those of a catastrophic nature.

Automobile

In the automobile area, the reinsurance program is arranged in one of two ways. The program may be split into (1) the fire, theft, physical damage section, and (2) the personal injury, third party liability section, and the two sections reinsured individually. Alternatively, the whole array of coverage may be reinsured in blanket fashion with one reinsurer. The former method is the older one, with excess of loss blanket coverage being a relatively new development. When the ceding company reinsures the individual sections separately, the normal practice is to utilize a quota share treaty for the fire,

[6]Henry T. Kramer, "The Effect of Reinsurance on Underwriting Policies and Practice," Read before the meeting of the American Management Association Briefing Session, New York, September 5, 1963, p. 11.

theft, and physical damage section and excess of loss for the personal injury and third party liability section.

The use of a quota share treaty for the automobile damage and theft area is a rather poor way to utilize one's reinsurance facilities. The vast majority of the losses are going to be less than $1 000, a figure which should be well within the ceding company's ability to retain for its own account. The danger of trading dollars is greater with this usage than with any other. All of these factors suggest that the insurer should be cautious when utilizing reinsurance in this manner. Periodic appraisals should be made in order to determine whether another form of reinsurance may be more appropiate.

The use of excess of loss reinsurance as a blanket coverage is the trend today. The reasons for this trend are apparent. Excess of loss reinsurance is easy to administer, thus reducing the operating costs to a minimum (to "half a girl" as one executive put it). Also, the most responsible insured may produce an insurer's worst claim and perhaps be an innocent party to the accident besides! The insurer cannot underwrite the individual risk but can only try to protect itself against an excessive loss. Finally, by using blanket coverage, the danger of "dollar swapping" is reduced.

General Liability

Included in this embracing "general liability" discussion on reinsurance practices are all kinds of liability which might be incurred by owners, landlords, tenents, contractors, employers, manufacturers, etc. As in automobile third party liability, it is impossible for underwriters to judge maximum possible loss in advance to any accurate degree. Further, the period from the time of the accident to final settlement often extends for a number of years. Because of these characteristics, excess of loss reinsurance is normally used, the retention being set in relation to the insurer's financial strength. It is not unusual for the same excess of loss contract to cover all of the third party liability written by the primary insurer, including the automobile risk.

Ocean Marine

In the ocean marine area, the reinsurance practices vary according to whether hull or cargo business is being reinsured. The overall marine account may have a catastrophe cover in the form of an excess of loss contract. The underlying retention of this catastrophe cover is set at the maximum underwriting limit for the Class A Hull (the most favorable hull risk). This cover will apply to both the hull and cargo accounts to provide protection against large losses on accumulations arising from collision, storage on quay-side, etc.

The hull account normally will be protected by a surplus treaty, the retentions varying according to the class of hull to be reinsured. The cargo account normally will be protected by a "working" excess of loss contract with the retention set relatively low. The normal operation of a cargo vessel is to make several stops per trip, dropping off some cargo and taking on more, the insurance on which has been arranged by the shipping agent. It is extremely difficult for the underwriter to determine exactly how much liability he will have on any one vessel at any one time, except at the outset of the voyage. It is, therefore, equally difficult to establish levels of retention for cession under a surplus treaty. Excess of loss reinsurance furnishes a nice answer to this otherwise ticklish problem.

Inland Marine

The normal reinsurance practice covering an insurer's inland marine account is the use of a working excess of loss contract, but occasionally peaks of exposure need to be reduced by use of a surplus facility which has multi-line capacity.

Burglary and Theft

As with the automobile reinsurance practices, burglary and theft insurers utilize two methods of meeting their reinsurance needs, depending upon their size. The majority of losses in this line are limited to relatively moderate amounts. Insurers with a respectable amount of surplus find that they can base their underwriting upon absorbing such losses. They protect themselves with excess of loss reinsurance against losses that exceed the moderate limit.

The more modest burglary and theft insurer whose volume in this class is insufficient to justify the attitude of absorbing the moderate losses normally will have a surplus treaty. This arrangement effectively reduces the commitment of the ceding company and allows it to protect its small volume by limiting its exposure to loss. As soon as the premium volume gets of sufficient size to absorb the majority of the losses experienced in this class, it is advantageous for the surplus to be dropped and to rely solely on the excess.

Fidelity and Surety

Because of the varying reinsurance needs of the bonding insurer, as compared to property and liability classes, this area of reinsurance presents a particularly interesting set of situations. The reinsurance needs of the fidelity-surety insurer can be placed in six basic categories.[7]

[7]Vincent J. McCarthy, *Fidelity and Surety Reinsurance*, (New York: Insurance Institute of America, 1945). See for an excellent study on the subject.

(1) As with any insurer, the bonding insurer wants its reinsurance to limit the net retention to an amount commensurate with financial capacity, general underwriting policy, and volume of business.

(2) There is a government limitation upon the amount the bonding insurer may retain net for its own account, i.e., after all reinsurance coverage has been subtracted. The Treasury Department requirement is that no company authorized to execute bonds in favor of the United States is allowed to assume, net, on a single risk an amount exceeding ten percent of its combined capital and surplus. The various states also have requirements of their own which must be considered.

(3) Fidelity-surety insurers also utilize their reinsurance to avoid an accumulation of liability on individual principals. Such accumulation is well illustrated by warehouse bonds which are required in great numbers and which can aggregate huge values on the part of an individual firm.

(4) The bonding insurer also finds that its reinsurance arrangements must provide a method of avoiding an accumulation of liability in certain classes of bonds. The bonding insurer utilizes reinsurance to provide a balance among the various types of bonds similar to the way an investor balances his investment portfolio between the various types and grades of stocks and bonds.

(5) One of the primary characteristics of the bonding class is that wide fluctuations in experience can be expected as the rule rather than the exception. In the other lines of insurance, the catastrophe hazards are fires, hurricanes, earthquakes, hailstorms, etc. The bonding catastrophe hazard is that of economic depression. The effects of a bonding catastrophe, unlike a fire conflagration or hurricane which affects only one or a few cities or areas, is nationwide or worldwide, causing almost all surety insurers to experience high loss ratios on many classes of bonds. As a result, the fidelity and surety insurer often has few profitable areas to help balance his catastrophe losses as do insurers of other lines of business.

(6) Finally, the surety insurer sometimes utilizes its reinsurance to transfer the risk on bonds of poor or uncertain quality.

Because of the wide variations and unusual reinsurance demands made on the part of the primary insurer in this area, there is a wide variation of reinsurance programs. However, the predominance of practice is to use a treaty form, normally surplus, in order to limit to a definite amount the liability assumed net by the ceding company and yet provide flexibility in the amount of reinsurance. On top of the treaty is a catastrophe cover in the form of either excess of loss or excess of loss ratio, the excess of loss being the most popular. In certain instances where the insurer is of sufficient magnitude, the underlying treaty is dropped completely; and the excess of loss contract is the sole component of the reinsurance program.

Personal Accident

The personal accident policy is a benefit policy with definite sums payable for specific injuries. The primary insurer normally utilizes only excess of loss with the retention set at the benefit payable for one or more lives. This effectively limits the ceding company's maximum possible loss on any one occurrence to the amount payable for the loss of the specified number of lives. As with the other classes of businss where the majority of losses are of a small nature, an underlying treaty may be used, but the insurer must be careful to avoid simply trading dollars with its reinsurer.

Workmen's Compensation

The workmen's compensation policy is divided into two sections in order to make it more manageable for analysis of reinsurance practices: (1) definite sums for medical and compensation per accident to be paid to the employees as dictated by state statutes, and (2) the employer's legal liability in lieu of these amounts. The primary insurer may reinsure under an excess of loss contract with the retention set at the benefit payable for loss of any one life extending up to $40,000 (as in the case of stock insurers who have the Workmen's Compensation Reinsurance Bureau which acts as an excess reinsurer above this amount) or the maximum benefit payable for any person. The mutual insurer commonly has an excess of loss contract which will absorb losses above the retention of the normal maximum benefit payable for any one life.

Accumulation is relatively easy to assess. This is done by an analysis of the working conditions provided by the employer and the number of employees working in the area or space so provided. The big problem and prime function of workmen's compensation reinsurance lies in unlimited medical benefits for permanent partial or total disability. One permanent total disability can equal the cost of twenty fatalities and often does. It is not uncommon in this area to find the larger insurers, both stock and mutual, requiring several layers of excess of loss coverage.

Hail

In order to answer the needs of the hail insurer as closely as possible, an interesting array of reinsurance agreements have been introduced. A primary method among the multitude of farm mutuals which write this business is to use excess of loss with the retention set at a certain amount of loss per township or county. Those insurers who are not large enough to assume liability alone for the full amount of the net retention find that a quota share treaty splits the liability up nicely. The percentage reinsured under the quota share treaty is gradually reduced over a period of time until the ceding company finally assumes the full burden of the underlying retention. This evolution is known as "growing into the excess." Facultative reinsurance is also used to reduce the commitment in any one county or township.

Another method of protecting the crop hail insurer is the use of the excess of loss ratio contract. The advantage this form of excess offers over excess of loss is due to the difficulties which arise in determining just where one hail storm stopped and another began. The determination of "one event" is necessary when an excess of a fixed amount is used in the straight excess of loss contract. Various systems have been applied in an attempt to successfully establish a single loss which is equally just to both parties, e.g., by time period or by geographical area. These systems often fail to avoid dissention between the parties. Excess of loss ratio avoids this difficulty by enabling the ceding company to regulate the results of the entire year's operation as a unit, thereby establishing a reinsuring base upon which equitable settlements can be made with relative ease.

An interesting development in the hail reinsurance area is the surplus township reinsurance agreement. In this form of reinsurance, the reinsurer accepts the surplus amount of hail liability written by the ceding company in each township over its retention. The reinsurer's limits of liability are specific amounts per township. The reinsurer then shares in the premium and losses in a direct proportion to the amount of liability reinsured per township. While this limits the maximum loss exposure in any one township, it does not provide complete heavy loss protection in the event two or more townships are involved in one storm.

Packages

Probably one of the most pressing reinsurance problems of the primary insurer and reinsurer alike today is how to most effectively reinsure the package policies which are representing an ever-increasing portion of the insurer's premium income. Basically these policies embody two distinct types of insurance cover: property insurance and liability insurance. In the past, these sections were either insured by two separate companies or if one company, in two or more different policies. As a result, each individual portion was underwritten, rated, a retention set, and reinsured. There was a definite premium charge for each cover and each portion received individual scrutiny, thereby enabling each to be equitably reinsured under a different reinsurance agreement.

The problem arises when the insurer starts offering both of these coverages in a package with one premium covering both sections. This practice at first glance seems not to be such a great problem. All the ceding company has to do is to break up the premium between sections. It can then reinsure each section separately as it has been doing in the past, the reinsurance premium being based upon an equitable breakdown of the original premium. An element enters into the computation of the premium, however, which was absent earlier, a discount for purchasing the entire coverage from one insurer. This means that this discount must then be broken down between sections. Is this discount broken down in the same ratio as the premium, or is the majority of it taken out of the most profitable, or the only profitable, section? Any answer to this question might be discriminating against one reinsurer in favor of another.

The discount breakdown problem may be relatively easy to solve in order to give an equitable portion of the premium to all parties concerned. The question of equitability at this point is so uncertain that when the primary insurer starts underwriting on an account basis rather than a risk basis, equitability becomes a serious question. The very basis of the package policy and its strong selling point emphasized by the agent is that it makes no difference whether one "small" area of the prospect's insurance history has been rather bleak or not. The "underwriters at the home office will take into account the rest of the areas which have been profitable and issue the policy at the standard rate and discount." It is thus easy to see that quickly the picture will become so foggy that no one, including the reinsurers, will know whether they are really receiving an equitable portion of the premium.

The problem is further accentuated if two different reinsurers are used, which is not uncommon at all. If one reinsurer has both coverages, the problem would tend to be not quite so serious, for one would balance out the other. With two reinsurers, however, all each would know is that they are not receiving their just share of the premium, for they might be losing money while the other is making a nice profit. Or maybe: they are losing more money than the other reinsurer.

A further factor, that of cost, becomes even of greater importance in reinsurance of packages. The normal rates are discounted fifteen percent, or possibly more, in order to induce the insured to buy the package. No sane company can really anticipate a better loss ratio than when the same account was covered less broadly under specific policies. The fifteen percent discount must be saved somewhere, and the cost off reinsurance and its administration is not exempt from cost-cutting activities.

To find at least a partial answer to the cost problem, not only the direct reinsurance costs, but also the indirect reinsurance costs (administrative costs) must be considered. Both of these cost areas must be reduced to a minimum. Because of the high costs associated with successfully placing a commercial package on the books, particularly a large one, an insurer cannot afford to cede 75 to 90 percent of the liability to reinsurers. The reinsurance commission received will just not cover the high costs. Because of these considerations, an excess of loss contract is normally selected as the reinsurance coverage for the entire package accepted by the department.

The blanket excess of loss coverage for package policies is fine for the larger insurer whose financial strength is sufficient to retain net for its own account the entire underlying retention, and yet establish the level of the retention high enough to keep the cost of the coverage within reason. The smaller insurer is not large enough to retain the whole of the underlying retention unless the net retention is so low that it costs too much. The only relief to the insurer in this position is to set up some form of underlying treaty in order to break down the ceding company's retention into bite-sized chunks. Since package business presently is not overly profitable, a surplus treaty which allows the ceding company to retain a larger portion of the profits than do the other forms of treaty reinsurance seems to be the best answer. There is a definite disadvantage associated with the use of a surplus treaty in this case. The handling and administrative costs associated with a surplus treaty introduce into the picture just what the insurer is trying to avoid, more cost. Unless there is more profit to be made than it will cost, the surplus treaty must not even be considered. With profits being as elusive as they are, the willingness of a reinsurer to accept a surplus treaty is another thing again.

The quota share treaty offers another alternative to the primary insurer. The administration costs of this form of treaty are relatively low; however, a larger portion of the profits will be passed on to the reinsurer than under the surplus form. The ceding company is in a better bargaining position when using quota share. As a result, it can probably get a larger reinsurance commission with which to meet the higher costs of package insurance and/or negotiate a lower rate on the excess coverage. The answer to this problem will, of course, vary from insurer to insurer, each one basing its decision upon the many variables that enter into its individual situation at the time.

SETTING YOUR NET RETENTION

One of the most critical areas in establishing a reinsurance program which maximizes benefits at a minimum of cost is that of setting the retention. The level of retention is critical for both quota share and surplus treaties, if utilized, and especially so for excess of loss coverage. Net retention can be defined as the unreinsured liability or loss, according to the kind of reinsurance contract concerned. An attempt has been made in this section to isolate and set down in as definite a manner as possible the primary factors which should be considered when establishing the net retention. It would be naive indeed to attempt to set out any hard and fast rules for setting the retention for any individual company because of the high degree of subjective reasoning necessary for a satisfactory solution to the problem. It is possible, however, to set out general, well-recognized points to consider when setting the retention.

General Considerations

There are basic considerations when setting the retention which apply to all forms of reinsurance. These conditions are the ones which have to be satisfied no matter what type of retention is being set, a percentage for a quota share, or dollar amounts for the surplus and excess of loss. These basic considerations are first discussed here, followed by more specific considerations for setting a retention for each individual form. There are six basic considerations: (1) management attitudes, (2) class or blanket reinsurance, (3) size of insurer, (4) class of insureds, (5) territory, and (6) cost.

Management Attitudes. Since it is management which finally decides just what the net retention is going to be, management's attitude toward risk bearing is definitely going to be reflected in their decision. It is in this area that management decides just how large a loss they "feel" they can stand, i.e., the size of losses the surplus can absorb without jeopardizing the well-being of the company.

Also important in this area is management's attitude toward the estimation of the Probable Maximum Loss (PML) in property insurance. It is partially upon the PML estimate that the primary underwriter bases his decision as to whether or not to accept a proposal and how much to retain for his own account. Management who will accept a PML estimate of ten percent had better have a lower retention than one whose net retained line is based upon a "nothing less than 25 percent" PML, even if the inspectors swear by the ground upon which they stand that it is "the" loss-proof risk. It is a well recognized fact that impossible losses do occur, and the underwriter who takes this into consideration in rating can safely get by with a higher retention.

Class Reinsurance or Blanket Reinsurance. As discussed earlier, class reinsurance is individual reinsurance coverage for each class of business written by the primary insurer. Blanket reinsuance is a single reinsurance cover applying to two or more classes of business. Normally when class reinsurance is used, the net retentions are set conservatively; for this coverage is used more actively to supplement underwriting. With blanket reinsurance, the net retention is geared to the over-all operation of the departments concerned rather than to the operations of any one department. A higher retention can be set because of the broader premium base and greater stability in results.

Size of Insurer. The size of the insurer definitely affects the amount of liability it can absorb on any one risk. Generally, the larger the insurer, the higher the retention. Size can be measured by premium volume or by assets. For reinsurance purposes, the measure of size is by premium volume. It is upon premium volume that the satisfaction of current obligations rests; therefore the ceding company cannot afford to be exposed to such an extent that a loss or series of losses can absorb too large a portion of its premium volume for that class or area.

Reinsurance and the net retention also have important effects upon the insurer's surplus. The effect of utilizing reinsurance, normally quota share, for the purpose of financing surplus for an extended period of time normally is not in the best interests of the company, unless it is practicing reciprocity which will reduce the net reinsurance cost. Without reciprocity, a large share of the profits on the business are passed on to the reinsurers which could be retained by the ceding company.

Class of Insureds. The class or type of risk selected by the insurer can have a definite effect upon the amount of liability retained. If the insurer's market is primarily in the substandard risk category, it is pretty certain that its retention will be relatively low in order to keep its exposure on any one risk limited. On the other hand, an insurer who writes only the cream of the business can be expected to have a relatively high retention.

Territory. The effect of the geographical area to be covered on the net retention is obvious. A propery insurer might have a different level of retention in the hurricane belt than he would in other areas relatively free from this hazard. Further, an insurer might have a lower retention in an area where its premium volume is small than it would have in another area where a substantial volume has been developed.

Cost. To many executives, all of the preceding discussion is good for theoreticians, students, and for speech material. When it comes down to the line, they feel the major factor is cost. Management is going to set its retention at a level it can afford. They might want the Rolls Royce, but for the present, they have to be satisfied with a lesser vehicle. Costs in the reinsurance area are particularly hard to measure because of the difficulty of comparing cost to value, particularly when heterogeneous units are involved. It is said that generally, the treaty form of reinsurance is more expensive than the excess form. However, in terms of value, which of these is most expensive? This is a difficult question to answer because there is some overlapping of functions between the two forms, but each one performs some functions the other does not.

A point ought to be made here about Lloyd's, London. Because of the organization of the various syndicate underwriters there, only one, or a very few underwriters at the most, act as "leaders" in the various lines of business. It is to these "leaders" that the Lloyd's Brokers go on the outset. The "leader's" function is to initially underwrite the risk, assign a rate, and assume a portion of the liability. If an insurer in its quest for stirring up competition to lower cost asks for quotes from two Lloyd's Brokers, in all probability, the same "leader" will be making the quote presented to the insurer by the different brokers. The net result of all of this maneuvering, particularly if several brokers are consulted, is the consternation of the Lloyd's underwriter concerned. The results are often his refusing to write the risk at the original rate quoted.

The best policy the primary insurer can follow when dealing with Lloyd's, London, is to select a broker with care and then be confident that he will get the best quote possible. The broker is far more concerned than the underwriter with how competitive Lloyd's is. The competent broker will therefore get the best quote he can. Then the way to get a Lloyd's rate reduced, if such is possible, is to request another bid by the same broker.

Another area which has a great effect upon the reinsurance rate is the company experience in the last five years. Excellent or poor experience alone is enough to lower or raise the rate, initially. The ultimate cost, however, is determined by the company experience during the term of the reinsurance agreement.

The final direct cost factor to be considered is that of the uncertainty of the ceding company's future experience. If the insurer is young with little past experience upon which to base a rate, one can expect that the cost will be more at the outset. The risk on the part of the reinsurer is greater due to the uncertanties involved. The same holds true if fundamental changes were made in underwriting policies, or if the proposed reinsurance is to cover a new policy or entry into a new area.

Another area of cost consideration is in the costs of administration associated with the various forms of reinsurance, the indirect costs. Because of the difficulty of accurately determining just how much of the overhead expenses can be attributed to the handling of the reinsurance program, indirect reinsurance costs are often ignored. It is important however, that these costs be considered. As indirect costs have little affect on the setting of the retention, they are discussed as an integral part of the chapters concerning the various reinsurance agreements.

Specific Considerations — Quota Share Treaty

The general considerations enumerated above play the predominant role in setting the percentage retention for a quota share treaty. The financial needs of the ceding company basically determine just how large a share will be retained. Generally, the smaller the surplus available for meeting the immediate acquisition expenses, the greater will be the percentage ceded. The retention will be smaller in order to free more cash, via the ceding commission, with which to meet expenses.

Another consideration is simply to reduce the primary insurer's commitment per risk to proper proportions. The size of the retention is, of course, a result of a combination of such factors as premium volume, size of surplus, and the general belief that quota share should be used by the primary insurer when entering a new area or class of business. There is a trend toward blanket reinsurance to cover the package policies. The blanket coverage is a working excess of loss contract. The cost factor of the excess is a vital consideration. The smaller insurers will find it difficult to retain for their own account the underlying retention on an excess contract necessary on the excess to make such a plan economically feasible. An example of how the relative cost of the working excess of loss increases as the net retention is lowered will bring this "squeeze" on the smaller insurer into focus:

Table VI

A COMPARISON OF RELATIVE COSTS OF A "WORKING" EXCESS OF LOSS CONTRACT AT VARYING LIMITS OF NET RETENTION[A]

LOSS CLASS	TOTAL LOSSES PER CLASS	BURNING COST	LOSS RATE[B] LOADING	LOADING AS % OF PREMIUM
More than				
$ 2,000	$1,960,000	$392,000	$168,000	3.4%
4,000	1,288,000	257,600	111,400	2.2
6,000	756,000	151,200	64,800	1.3
8,000	364,000	72,800	31,200	0.6
10,000	224,000	44,800	19,200	0.4
12,000	140,000	28,000	12,000	0.2
14,000	112,000	22,400	9,600	0.2

[A]The figures are for a period of five years, the average loss ratio assumed is 56% total five year premium volume assumed is $5,000,000.

[B]This rate is based upon the net retention being set at the lower limit of each class for which the rate is computed. The loading factor is 100/70.

From the table, it can be seen that the percentage increase in the cost of excess loss coverage increases as the net retention is lowered. The column of "Loading as a percent of premium" shows the relative cost of the cover in relation to a commom base, the premium income. This cost comparison assumes even greater importance when one recalls that this cost will have to be paid out of profits. An insurer would have to make initially in excess of 3.4 percent profit in order to merely break even if his retention is set at $2,000 in the example. In this case, in order to have a net return of 5 percent before taxes to the stockholder, the company would have to make an underwriting profit of 8.4 percent.

The solution to this squeeze between the desire for such a cover and the cost of the cover is to set the net retention for the excess of loss cover at a level where the cost is not prohibitive. The retention of $10,000 in the example might be chosen. This would cost 0.4 percent. For the smaller insurer, however, to be exposed to the extent of $10,000 on any one loss is almost as bad as paying the 3.4 percent charge. As a result, the insurer may add a treaty which will reduce its exposure to more manageable proportions. Because of the administration cost factor between the various forms of treaty reinsurance, the insurer has to settle on a form which will add as little to his overhead costs as possible. He is already spending 0.4 percent for the excess of loss coverage. While 0.4 percent does not appear too great, it assumes a different magnitude when one considers that most insurers have at best fourteen percent to cover all of their costs except acquisition (35 percent – 18 percent acquisition – 3 percent premium tax). In many instances, the insurer has settled upon the quota share treaty as offering the best solution to the problem of reducing the net retention without increasing the cost of reinsurance to uneconomic proportions.

Specific Considerations — Surplus Treaty

In addition to the general considerations enumerated earlier, there are two more factors which should be taken into consideration when establishing the net retention for a surplus treaty. The net retention should be set at a level which (1) provides risk size homogeneity and (2) takes into consideration the ratio between the maximum exposure under the proposed retention and the estimated premium income of the class to be covered.

Homogeneity. The basic function of the surplus treaty is to provide risk size homogeneity to the ceding company. The retention has to be set so as to limit the variation between the average size of risk insured in each class to such a degree that the Law of Large Numbers is allowed to function in an efficient manner. The more extreme the the variation between the sizes of the risks insured and the average risk insured, the greater will be the fluctuations of actual experience from expected experience.

Because of the inherent characteristic of selection against the reinsurer in the surplus treaty, reinsurers take care to see that the level of retention is set at an equitable level. A reinsurer will not, under normal circumstances, assume any liability under a surplus treaty unless the retentions are so set that the reinsurer will get (1) an equitable share of the good risk as well as the bad ones, and (2) a sufficient spread, by number of risks reinsured, for the efficient operation of the Law of Large Numbers.

Ratio of Estimated Premium Income to MPL. The ratio of estimated premium income to maximum possible loss is of prime importance to both the primary insurer and the reinsurer. In fact, if any one rule or method of behavior could be called "the" rule of first surplus reinsurance, it would probably be this one: the maximum possible loss under the treaty must not exceed the estimated premium income.[8] To the primary insurer, this rule means that exposure, or net retained liability, must not exceed the estimated net premium income, after allowance for expenses. To the reinsurer, the rule means that the estimated premium income under the treaty must exceed its share of the liability assumed under the treaty. Generally, if exposure does exceed premium income, the underwriter can expect to experience a loss under the treaty in the long run.

This ratio between the estimated premium income and the maximum possible loss is used to determine the "balance" of a treaty. A treaty is said to be unbalanced when this ratio is below the standards set by the individual underwriter concerned, but in no case less than 1.0. Granted, this certainly is a poor way to define balance, but the standards vary to such an extent that to say anything other than this would be misleading.

In order to clarify this picture of the concept of treaty balance and to skirt disaster at the same time, a generalization such as the following is useful. Normally everyone in the business will agree that a ratio of less than one (premiun income divided by maximum possible loss) indicates that the treaty is unbalanced. The gray area where a treaty becomes "barely balanced" in the property field is somewhere between the ratio of one to the ratio of five for a young, relatively small, but growth-minded company. The more aggressive underwriters will be closer to a ratio of one, and the more conservative ones will tend to favor a ratio of five. For older property companies who have a more respectable premium volume, the treaty would be considered "barely" balanced between a ratio of five to a ratio of ten and well balanced at twenty.

The higher the ratio is, the better balanced the treaty. Assuming a satisfactory loss ratio, the better balanced the treaty the more attractive it is to the reinsurers. As an indication of ratios that have been attained by some companies and groups, ratios in excess of fifty are not unusual, and those greater than one hundred are occasionally reached. As a company's premium volume grows, its average size of risk remains relatively stable, thereby increasing the ratio. The rise in premium volume does not necessarily mean that the company is insuring larger risks but rather a larger number of the same sized risks. The ceding company can vary the ratio also by varying the type and/or class(es) of business which are included in the treaty and also by varying the net retention.

[8]This does not mean that this is not a consideration for the other areas of reinsurance, but rather that it is the primary rule in first surplus reinsurance which *must* not be disregarded.

Specific Considerations — Excess of Loss

One of the most difficult reinsurance decisions the preimary insurer has to make is setting the level of the net retention for the excess of loss coverage. The problem is to obtain the protection required and yet not drain off any more of the premium dollar than is absolutely necessary. In the past, the typical reinsurance program was composed of a treaty of some form and catastrophe coverage in the form of an excess of loss contract. However, the validity of using a treaty as well as the excess contract is being seriously questioned. As a consequence, the net retention for the excess of loss coverage for Typical Insurance Company has been slowly dropping, making the treaty smaller and smaller. In many instances, the treaty has disappeared all together. The end result of this trend is that the company has a two or more layer excess of loss reinsurance program, the bottom layer being what is known as a "working" excess and the upper layers remaining a catastrophe cover.

The name "working excess" reflects the fact that the excess has replaced a treaty which was actively working at the business of every day claims, not being solely restricted to those of a catastrophic nature. A better name for such an excess of loss contract is "exposed" rather than "working," and "unexposed" rather than "catastrophe." Although either name is acceptable, the suggested names deal with their fundamental function. The name "exposed" comes from the characteristic that the lower limit of the excess, the ceding company's net retention, is set within the limits of the ceding company's maximum underwriting limits on any one risk. It is, therefore, "exposed" to the amount of the difference between the reinsurance limit and the ceding company's maximum underwriting limit. "Exposed" relates to the position of the reinsurer being such that it can be liable for a portion of loss by a single insured. "Unexposed" relates to the position of the reinsurer being such that it can only become liable for a portion of a loss when two or more insureds are involved in the same loss.

The following discussion of the methods of settling the net retention for excess of loss contracts is broken down into those methods concerned with the retention of the exposed excess and those methods concerned with the retention on the unexposed excess.

Methods of Setting the Retention for an Exposed Excess. As pointed out earlier, the lower the net retention is placed, the greater the exposure and the more expensive it becomes. The ideal place for the limit has been vaguely stated by reinsurers as being high enough so as not to be involved in the majority of the claims and yet low enough to keep the ceding company from being too greatly exposed in any one occurrence. The area where the bulk of the premium is absorbed by claims should be retained by the insurer in order to avoid "dollar swapping." Fundamentally then, the theory is that the ceding company should assume as much risk as soundly possible. Risk assumption is the insurer's business. In order to assume risk successfully, an insurer protects itself from severe fluctuations in experience by setting the retention where loss predictability declines rapidly. Basically, there appear to be three methods for placing the retention on an exposed excess of loss contract; the Variation in Loss Ratio Method, the Loss Frequency Method, and the Integrated Cost Method.

Variation in Loss Ratio Method: The basic consideration of the Variation in Loss Ratio Method is that the entire area of high loss frequency should be retained by the primary insurer. The chance of variation between expected and actual experience is slight in this area. The insurer who passes premium dollars that will be needed to meet these predictable claims is trading dollars with the reinsurer. The size of losses up to a certain point is predictable. The net retention should be set where predictability falls off for maximum risk assumption by the insurer commensurate with safety to the policyholders.

The actual procedure followed in utilizing this method is to divide the last ten years' loss experience into classes according to size, e.g., $2,000 and less, $2,001 to $4,000, etc.). These losses are then computed as a percentage of that year's earned premium income. After this calculation has been made, the average loss per class for the ten years can be obtained. The average loss thus computed is used as the base for a comparison of the yearly variation of loss experience.

The subjective reasoning steps in here. A point must be established beyond which the variation from the average is enough to be considered unpredictable – where the risk, in the estimation of management, is greater than is in the best interests of the policyholders and/or the shareholders. For example, a variation of five percent from the ten years' average loss ratio may be established as that point. However, management may feel that nothing is predictable if the estimate is couched in a "plus or minus five percent" phrase; so they may settle on a variation cutoff point of two percent. Still another group of executives may come along, after looking at the pro's and con's of both the five percent and the two percent decisions, may decide that their surplus is of such magnitude that they can easily absorb variations up to seven percent without endangering their financial position. The interesting thing is that some little, growth-minded company, with a threadbare surplus but aggressive management, may come along and agree with the seven percent decision, thus emphasizing the many variables that enter into even this relatively minor decision.

Tables VII and VIII have been drawn up as an example of how one might go about using this method. The results obtained from analyzing the tables, using a standard "not more than five percent variation," would be the establishment of the retention around $6,000.

Table VII

LOSSES AS PERCENTAGE OF EARNED PREMIUM PER YEAR

CLASS	SIZE OF LOSSES	1	2	3	4	5	6	7	8	9	10	AVERAGE
1	$ 2,000 & Less	20	21	20	20	19	20	20	21	20	20	20.1
2	2,000 - 3,999	16	15	15	16	16	15	15	15	16	16	15.6
3	4,000 - 5,999	12	12	11	11	12	12	11	12	11	11	11.5
4	6,000 - 7,999	6	5	7	6	7	5	6	6	6	7	6.1
5	8,000 - 9,999	4	2	5	7	2	1	9	3	4	2	3.8
6	10,000 - 11,999	3	7	1	2	5	1	3	4	1	3	3.0
7	12,000 - 13,999	2	5	0	1	2	4	0	2	1	3	2.0
8	14,000 & Above	1	0	2	0	0	0	4	0	0	0	0.7
TOTAL LOSS RATIO		64	67	61	63	63	60	67	63	59	62	62.8

The Loss Frequency Method: Proponents of the Loss Frequency Method of establishing the net retention for an exposed excess of loss contract also have as their basic postulate that the entire area of high loss frequency should be assumed by the primary insurer. This, they say, is the more efficient way to avoid swapping dollars with the reinsurer; for this is the area in which the bulk of the claim dollar is absorbed. In many ways, both methods cover the same considerations; and it is probably to the advantage of the insurer to investigate both areas before setting the retention.

The procedure for setting up the Loss Frequency Method is to determine the loss frequency in relation to total losses per $1,000 units. The point where the frequency begins to fall off appreciably is approximately where the underlying limit for the excess should be set. The following example has been included to demonstrate how this method might be set up. Using this method, the retention should be set somewhere around $8,000. In this example, the two methods differ considerably in order to bring out a fundamental difference between the two. One is volume of losses, and the other is frequency of losses.

TABLE VIII

VARIATION IN LOSS RATIO PER CLASS PER YEAR IN RELATION TO THE AVERAGE LOSS RATIO PER CLASS

CLASS	AVG. LOSS RATIO	1	2	3	4	5	6	7	8	9	10
1	20.1%	0.5%	4.5%	0.5%	0.5%	5.4%	0.5%	0.5%	4.5%	0.5%	0.5%
2	15.6	2.8	4.0	4.0	2.8	2.8	4.0	4.0	4.0	2.8	2.8
3	11.5	4.2	4.2	4.2	4.2	4.2	4.2	4.2	4.2	4.2	4.2
4	6.1	1.7	18.0	14.5	1.7	14.5	18.0	18.0	1.7	1.7	14.5
5	3.8	5.0	47.5	31.8	84.0	47.5	73.7	237.0	21.0	5.0	47.5
6	3.0	---	233.0	67.0	33.0	67.0	67.0	---	33.0	67.0	---
7	2.0	---	150.0	100.0	50.0	---	100.0	100.0	---	50.0	50.0
8	0.7	41.1	100.0	285.0	100.0	100.0	100.0	557.0	100.0	100.0	100.0

TABLE IX

LOSS FREQUENCY EXPERIENCE PER $1,000 OF CLAIMS

SIZE OF LOSSES	PERCENT OF TOTAL LOSSES[A]
Less than $ 2,000	30%
$ 2,000 to 3,999	24
4,000 to 5,999	19
6,000 to 7,999	14
8,000 to 9,999	5
10,000 to 11,999	3
12,000 to 13,999	1
14,000 and above	4

[A]Average number of the company's last fire year's experience.

Under normal circumstances, one would not expect to have these two methods yield results as widely separated as in the example.

The Integrated Cost Method: The Integrated Cost Method is a retention setting system which yields the retention levels of least cost for an integrated reinsurance program composed of a surplus or quota share treaty and excess of loss coverage. It is a method which gives an overall picture of the combined coverages and integrates them into the most effective coverage for the least cost. The Integrated Cost Method is based upon the recognition that up to a certain retention, treaty reinsurance is less costly than excess of loss. The Integrated Cost approach is designed to enable the primary insurer to pin-point the optimal retention so as to maximize value and minimize cost. This method can be adopted for use when only excess of loss coverage is used by substituting the cost of "self reinsuring" for the treaty cost curve.

The method consists basically of plotting two cost curves on the same table, the point of intersection being the point where the excess of loss retention should be set. The X axis is graduated in terms of percentage cost in relation to direct earned premiums, the Y axis being graduated in terms of various levels of retention. The treaty curve, Curve A in Table X, is plotted utilizing the following formula:[9]

[9]See the section "Determining the Cost of Your Reinsurance" (page 119) for a detailed discussion of this formula.

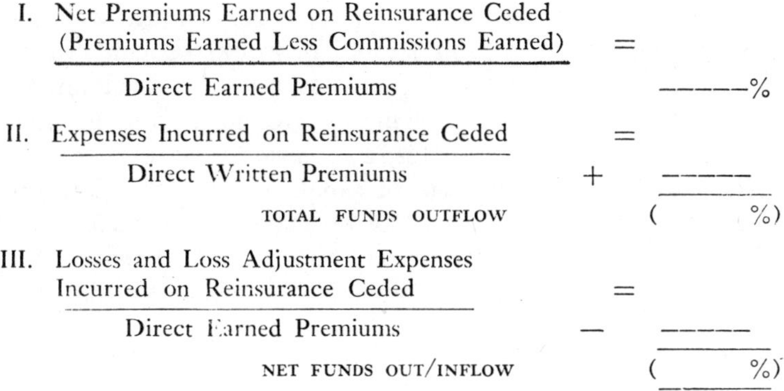

I. Net Premiums Earned on Reinsurance Ceded (Premiums Earned Less Commissions Earned) / Direct Earned Premiums = -----%

II. Expenses Incurred on Reinsurance Ceded / Direct Written Premiums = + -----

TOTAL FUNDS OUTFLOW (%)

III. Losses and Loss Adjustment Expenses Incurred on Reinsurance Ceded / Direct Earned Premiums = − -----

NET FUNDS OUT/INFLOW (%)

TABLE X

INTEGRATED COST OF REINSURANCE AT VARYING LEVELS OF RETENTION

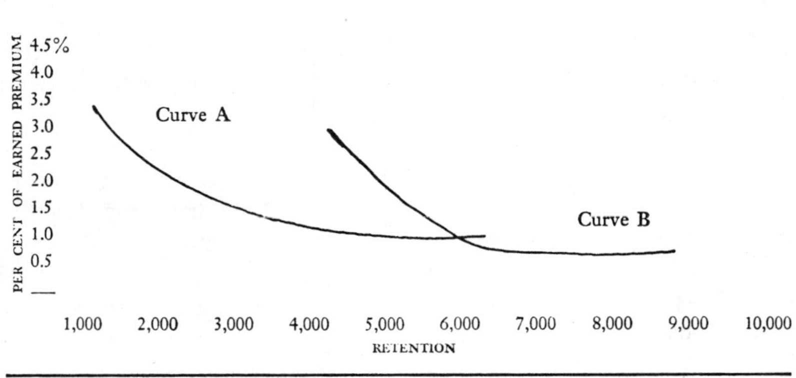

The shape of this curve will vary primarily as a result of (1) the costs of administration, (2) the type of treaty used, and (3) the various retentions set within the treaty, if it is a surplus.

The Excess of Loss Cost Curve, Curve B in Table X, is the percentage relation between the dollar volume of loading and earned premium income at the varying levels of retention. The formula that was used in determining the cost of the treaty is not applied here, as Burning Cost is a more accurate figure and easier to obtain than is the figure obtained by computing premiums ceded less recoveries in any one year. Since Burning Cost is pure cost of the coverage, the loading may be accurately stated as the effective cost to the ceding company. Because of this, the loading as a percentage of earned premium is used for determining the cost of an excess of loss contract in this method. The results of the use of the Integrated Cost Method would yield a presentation similar to Table X.

The retention in this example (Table X) for the excess of loss contract would be set around $6,500. It would probably be a good procedure to establish this point for several years back in order to determine the central level (the mean) around which the points fall during these years. By doing this, a retention level can be set that is at neither extreme of the range of points and which takes into consideration any trends which may be revealed by this process.

After the general level of retention has been determined by use of one or more of the above methods, the other general considerations should then be set alongside this decision to see whether they are satisfied by this retention. More than likely, it will have to be adjusted somewhat in order to match the criteria of the methods with cost, management attitudes, territory to be covered, etc.

Methods of Setting the Net Retention for an Unexposed Excess. As mentioned earlier, the unexposed excess of loss contract is designed to protect the ceding company from the ravages of a catastrophe or series of catastrophes. So long as there is reinsurance coverage to the lower limit of the catastrophe cover, the question of where to set the net retention is more academic than anything else. However, since there are some theories as to where to set this retention, a perusal of them might prove of interest.

In this area of retention setting, there are two methods, one simple and the other almost as simple; one is "old hat" and the other more sophisticated, i.e., the maximum underwriting limit and the Cushion Theory.

The old method of setting the retention for the catastrophe cover is to set it a the maximum underwriting limit for the line or lines of business to be covered by the contract. Since the question of whether a cover is truly a catastrophe cover or not is answered by determining whether it is exposed or unexposed, this method of setting the net retention appears quite logical and extrmely simple. However, this seems to be its fatal weakness – lack of sophistication; therefore, the Cushion Theory was developed.

The foundation upon which the Cushion Theory stands is that of limiting the loss ratio fluctuations. The primary function of excess of loss is to level out experience. This leveling is accomplished through the reinsurer absorbing violent fluctuations in the year they occur and the ceding company reimbursing the reinsurer for services rendered over the next five years. This effectively "spreads" the heavy losses over a period of time, thereby stabilizing the loss ratio. Since this is the primary purpose of the cover, why should this not be taken directly into consideration when setting the net retention for the cover? This is exactly what the Cushion Theory does.

The way one would go about utilizing this theory is to set down in an orderly manner the combined experience of the company for the last ten or so years. The area of profit, or the differences between one hundred percent and the combined loss and expense ratio for that year, is the "cushion" area, so to speak. This area represents a premium volume which would have to be absorbed by a loss before it can enter directly into surplus and leave the company showing a loss for the year. The larger this cushion area, the less critical is the need for setting a low underlying retention. The next step is to determine how large a loss would have to be in order to cause a noticeable fluctuation or reduction in the size of the cushion area. The figure thus obtained should be approximately where the net retention should be set, thereby limiting the amount of a single, heavy loss could move the loss ratio around in any one year. The following example is included in order to demonstrate just how this theory is designed to work.

As disclosed by Table XI, in years two and seven, a catastrophe or extremely large loss amounting to two percent of the earned premium income, or $1,000,000 (assuming a $50 million earned premium), would have completely erased any profit the company might have otherwise shown.

The point to consider is how large a loss is necessary to cause a noticeable fluctuation in experience. The average profit for the ten years outlined above is 4.8 percent. A loss which causes a fluctuation of ten percent of one hundred percent of the average profit (ten

TABLE XI

TEN YEAR SUMMARY OF EXPERIENCE
FOR COMPANY X

YEAR	LOSS RATIO (TO EARNED PREMIUM)	EXPENSE RATIO (TO EARNED PREMIUM)	PROFIT (CUSHION)
1	64%	32%	4%
2	67	31	2
3	61	30	9
4	63	34	3
5	63	32	5
6	60	33	7
7	67	31	2
8	63	32	5
9	59	34	7
10	62	34	4

percent being a fluctuation of .48 percent in experience) can be considered as causing a "noticeable" fluctuation. In dollar terms, this is a loss of $240,000. Utilizing the Cushion Theory, the reinsurance program should be designed to ensure that the company will not experience a loss in "any one occurance" which will cost the company more than $240,000.

Although only on rare occasions will the two methods of setting the retention for catastrophe cover outlined above agree, they each have their definite advantages. Probably, if the Cushion Theory yields a higher figure, the smaller insurer would be better off if it definitely limited its maximum exposure by utilizing the maximum underwriting limit method. Conversely, the larger the insurer might find by utilizing the Cushion Theory that it has not been assuming as much risk as it could assume with relative safety and would therefore prefer this method to the more conservative one. Thus, as with all general decision areas, the various factors affecting each individual situation will dictate the optimum solution. Each factor must be considered on its individual merits at the time, for there is no method yet devised which can forecast exactly what the proper level of retention should be. Further, until insurers start realizing a reasonable degree of underwriting profit, it is difficult to use the Cushion Theory in its strictest sense; however, it still provides an excellent bench mark.

When considering catastrophe protection, it must always be remembered that the objective of the program is to protect the loss ratio and/or the surplus from the effects of *all* shock losses during the year. The net retention should be set in such a manner as to enable the insurer to definately limit the net retained losses in any one year. Suppose the net retention is set at a flat $1,000,000 per occurrence, and the insurer's net premiums earned are $100,000,000. One catastrophe cannot move the loss ratio more than one percent. What if three catastrophe losses in excess of $1,000,000 were experienced in one year? The loss ratio would jump three percent. When the past history of the insurer reveals that characteristically it experiences a number of heavy losses each year, an aggregating net retention should be used. The insurer could then definitely limit its catastrophe net retention to $1,000,000 as in the example above.

SETTING THE UPPER LIMITS ON YOUR CATASTROPHE COVER

Just exactly how deep should an insurer's catastrophe protection be? The more protection an individual or firm has, the smaller are its chances of loss. As with the individual who has a point where he is "over insured," so does the insurer have a point where he is "over reinsured." This point, however, is particularly elusive. The criteria is how well the executives sleep at night, free from the nightmare of a financial foundation-shaking catastrophic loss. In certain instances, it might be true to say that the insurer should have all that it can afford; however, because the majority of insurers are operating in accordance with sound underwriting principles, the need for catastrophe cover is definitely limited to some reasonable level.

Due to the high level of subjectivity entering into this decision, beliefs as to just how to measure the adequacy of protection are widely varied and of such a general nature as to elude firm classification. However, generally speaking, it can be stated with relative security that an insurer of non-marine lines, which has an annual premium volume of less than $300,000, should have catastrophe protection for a loss of at least twice that amount. It does not take a good hurricane or hail storm long to accumulate $600,000 in losses. As the insurer's premium volume grows, the depth of catastrohpe coverage in relation to premium volume can be gradually reduced. The amount of reduction reflects the opinion as to what the total possible losses in a catastrophe could be in the areas concerned. For example, if extended coverage premiums for an insurer on the Eastern seaboard from Florida to Massachusetts were $10,000,000, it would probably be safe with a total catastrophe protection of $1,000,000, as it is hardly conceivable that ten percent of its insureds would be involved in any one catastrophe.

Another factor effecting the depth of catastrophe protection is the territorial spread of the business written. In the storm areas, the total amount of protection might be related to the total fire and extended coverage premium volume in each area. The same rule could also apply to heavily concentrated areas where the chance of a conflagration is relatively high. This does not mean, however, that there should necessarily be separate covers for each individual area with the limits set according to the premium volume in each one. It might well be that by establishing a blanket catastrophe cover for the whole company experience, the costs might be less and the protection more.

DETERMINING THE COST OF YOUR REINSURANCE

The importance of accurately determining the cost of reinsurance coverage is obvious; however, relatively few executives actually make a serious attempt at accurately determining what they are paying for their program. A reply one might receive when asking this question would be that it is the difference between the commission allowed on the premiums ceded and the acquisition and office expenses of the ceding company. For example, a primary insurer might receive a reinsurance commission of forty percent on their cessions while their business expenses are thirty-five percent. Thus, they believe their reinsurance is costing them nothing; in fact, they think they are making a five percent profit on the transaction. This is not strictly true because the reinsurer has to meet his expenses and make a profit; therefore, this amount is passed up profit and is justly considered an expense by the ceding company. It is evident, however, that this is a rather inadequate way to determine the cost of reinsurance coverage.

Although the preceding method does give the insurer a general idea as to how much its reinsurance is costing, there is another method, through relating it to earned premium income, which brings the cost into focus. There are two distinct advantages to this comparison. First, it is a percentage figure directly comparable to profit made by the ceding company on its total earned premium income. Secondly, it facilitates the comparison of reinsurance costs between insurers, assuming that this method or one similar to it, is utilized by other insurers.

Generally, the method is to add, expressed in percentage of premiums earned, net premiums earned on reinsurance ceded, plus incurred administration expenses on reinsurance ceded, and subtract all recoveries from the reinsurers. The result is the net balance between the percentage of outgo and percentage of recovery. Specifically, the formula may be stated as follows:

I. $\dfrac{\text{Net Premiums Earned on Reinsurance Ceded (Premiums Earned Less Commissions Earned)}}{\text{Direct Earned Premiums}}$ = ______%

II. $\dfrac{\text{Expenses Incurred on Reinsurance Ceded}}{\text{Direct Written Premiums}}$ = + ______

TOTAL FUNDS OUTFLOW (%)

III. $\dfrac{\text{Losses and Loss Adjustment Expenses Incurred on Reinsurance Ceded}}{\text{Direct Earned Premiums}}$ = − ______

NET FUNDS OUT/INFLOW (%)

The following example computation of the cost of a reinsurance treaty is included to facilitate a better understanding of the formula:

Assumptions:

1. Total Premiums Earned on Reinsurance Ceded	$100,000	
2. Reinsurance Commission Earned (40%)	40,000	
3. Net Premiums Earned on Reinsurance Ceded		$ 60,000
4. Direct Earned Premiums		1,000,000
5. Expenses Incurred on Reinsurance Ceded		5,000
6. Direct Written Premiums		1,200,000
7. Losses and Loss Adjustment Expenses Incurred on Reinsurance Ceded		50,000

I. $\dfrac{\$\ 60{,}000}{\$1{,}000{,}000} = 6.0\ \%$

+

II. $\dfrac{\$\ 5{,}000}{\$1{,}200{,}000} = 0.42$

Total Funds Outgo 6.42%

—

III. $\dfrac{\$\ 50{,}000}{\$1{,}000{,}000} = 5.00$

Net Funds Outgo 1.42%

The use of written and paid figures instead of earned and incurred figures would result in a distorted picture with the exception of the expense figure which shall be taken up later. Written premiums at any one time are only partially earned. In order to place everything into proper prospective, income and outgo must be measured in the periods in which they were earned, and not necessarily when they were received.

The expense portion which uses written figures instead of earned ones is not a violation of accounting principles. The expenses which are incurred in present operations are paid out of current income and should be so related. The indirect reinsurance expenses which include costs incurred in acquiring, setting up, maintaining, and operating the reinsurance program are part of the present operations and are, therefore, paid out of current income. The difficult part of this formula is determining exactly what these expenses are; however, it is essential for a concerted effort to be made to accurately assess these costs because of their tendency to creep, unnoticed, to higher and higher proportions.

Reinsurance is a necessary element in the insurance industry; therefore, the costs of reinsurance are justifiable costs of doing business. Insurers should take a careful look at their reinsurance costs to see whether they are getting a balance between value and cost. For an illustration of just what this balancing of value and cost could mean, a closer look at the earlier example is required.

In this example, the reinsurance coverage for the year cost this insurer 1.42 percent of its earned premium income. Although this does not sound like too much of an expense, another comparison reveals an interesting fact. The percentage figure established, 1.42 percent is direct profit which would have been made had the primary insurer assumed full liability for all of the risks ceded instead of reinsuring it. The results would have been, assuming the insurer makes an underwriting profit of five percent, a six percent profit. Although this is a relatively impressive increase in profits, it becomes even more so when one considers the percentage increase in profit, which in this case is twenty percent! To put it another way, the ceding company is paying better than twenty percent of its profits for a ten percent coverage of its risk, for the above example was based upon only a ten percent quota share treaty.[10]

REDUCING THE COST OF YOUR REINSURANCE

As a result of the strong competitive pressures and the current economic situation, costs are the all-important topic of conversation among executives of all industries today. The concern for costs in some businesses has led to the extreme of a paper-saving campaign. Reinsurance is an area which has not been free from cost-consciousness, but it has been more on the part of the reinsurer than the reinsured. What can be done by the reinsured in order to reduce the cost of reinsurance? There are two primary answers to this question, (1) the paper-saving aspects which bring considerable savings here and there, and (2) the programming aspects which by careful consideration can save thousands of dollars without sacrificing essential coverage. Although the former aspects are certainly of importance, they will be given a back seat here, for they are more of a departmental nature, while the programming aspects shall take priority. The following section is organized by forms of reinsurance agreements in an effort to determine what generally might be done in order to reduce the costs in each area.

[10]Obviously, there is another side of the picture. If the business ceded into the treaty were unprofitable, the ceding company would only compound its loss by retaining the portion ceded. The purpose of the example is to emphasize the need for accurately determining the cost of reinsurance coverage.

Cost Reduction — Facultative

The way to reduce the high cost of handling facultative reinsurance is to eliminate facultative cessions. Although this sounds rather absurd at first, it can be done to a considerable degree. The vehicle is the use of a Facultative Obligatory Treaty which gives the ceding company complete freedom, just as it would have without it. The ceding company, however, has the advantages of automatic cession whenever it deems that an individual risk needs to be reinsured. Although reinsurers shy away from this form because of its characteristics of adverse selection and insufficient spread, it can be obtained.

Cost Reduction — Surplus

The indirect costs associated with the use of the surplus treaty are relatively high. A cost saving device which has been introduced is to use a percentage system whereby each reinsurer has a percentage of one hundred percent of the treaty instead of having a reinsurer(s) per line. The normal procedure is to mark the daily reports with the percentage of reinsurance to be ceded instead of the amount of cession and reinsurance premium. The premium to the individual treaty reinsurer is easily determined by reference to this percentage. A further reduction in reinsurance costs under the surplus treaty can be obtained through the use of reciprocity. If used with intelligence and care, this practice can reduce considerably the net cost of reinsurance, assuming a basic underwriting profit.[11]

Cost Reduction — Excess of Loss

Because of the varying cost of excess of loss coverage as the level of net retention is varied, one of the most effective methods of reducing one's cost of excess reinsurance is to experiment with various retention limits to see which is least costly. One factor must always be kept in the foreground when experimenting in this manner. As the retention lowers, it replaces, normally, a portion of an underlying treaty; and as the retention rises, it must be replaced by a treaty unless the insurer is prepared to assume the area thus exposed. Consequently, along with considering strictly the cost of the cover, the insurer must also consider (1) the cost savings or loss over the treaty, and (2) the effects on surplus because of the financing aspects of a treaty.

The way one would go about making this comparison is to first select several possible retention levels. Then, with these retention lev-

[11]For a detailed discussion on the proper use of reciprocity, see Chapter VII, "The Art of Reciprocity," page 147.

els, review the gross experience over the last five years and determine the volume of losses in excess of each retention. The final step is to determine the cost at each of these levels by first multiplying by a loading factor similar to 100/70, then subtracting the burning cost to get the loading or cost figure. The loading factor should be based upon actual estimates by a reinsurer or broker. In order to firmly establish the relative cost, this loading should be divided by the earned premium income for the period; thus, resulting in a percentage figure which can be compared to profits, other costs, etc. An example of such a comparison is found in Table VI on page 107, and the discussion following the table is applicable to this section as well.

As mentioned earlier, the loading cost of the excess must not be considered alone. It must also be compared with the savings over whatever type of treaty it would replace or be replaced by. A further consideration would be how much strain would have been placed on surplus by the unearned premium reserve requirement during each of the periods being investigated had the proposed net retention been established.

TREATY VS. EXCESS OF LOSS

One of the many points of debate today is whether it is a sound practice to replace a treaty with an exposed or "working" excess of loss contract. Among the many advantages in favor of this replacement are the cost factors; i.e., (1) the administration or indirect costs of the excess of loss form are negligible; and (2) as a general rule, it actually costs less than the treaty it replaces. It is the intent of this section to outline the considerations effecting a decision of this nature.

Before progressing any further, it would be wise to set out the relatively well-recognized ground rules concerning the classes of insurance in which the excess of loss form can replace the treaty form without disrupting the effective protection of the ceding company. The following quote by C. E. Golding on this subject stakes out the boundaries quite nicely:[12]

> It appears to the writer that a sharp distinction ought to be maintained between these two contrasting methods of reinsuring by excess of loss. In those classes of business in which it is applicable as

[12]C. E. Golding, *The Law and Practice of Reinsurance*, (London: Buckley Press Ltd., 1954), p. 95.

> the sole means of cover, the claims arise from circumstances which are largely similar in character, no matter what the nature of the risk may be. For, though risks may and do vary in hazard, this affects the frequency rather than the cost of claims. It is therefore logical to determine a figure as the underlying retention applicable to all classes of risk alike, the higher risks being taken care of by the reinsurance rate. If however, such a method of fixed underlying retention were applied to business such as fire insurance, conditions are quite otherwise. The circumstances likely to give rise a claim vary very widely and hazardous risks possess not only a greater chance of claim but also a much greater potential cost. To apply the excess of loss method as the sole means of reinsuring fire business to which by its nature such a retention is quite unsuitable and which would very greatly restrict the ceding company's opportunities to underwrite its business on sound lines. As a conflagration cover used in addition to the surplus treaties and meant to apply to the ceding company's net retention, it is quite a suitable means of reinsuring, so as to set up a safeguard against the accidental accumulation of risk which, even with the most careful system of net limits, it is not always possible to avoid.

Thus, in order for an insurer to even start considering the sole use of excess of loss reinsurance, the classes of business to be protected must meet the following requirement: the risk insured must not vary widely in value although the hazard may vary to a great extent. The varying hazard will only affect the frequency of losses. In these classes, homogeneity is sufficiently established to allow for the efficient working of the Law of Large Numbers without the direct aid of reinsurance. In those areas where the value of the risks insured vary widely, the ability of reinsurance to produce size homogeneity is a distinct aid to satisfactory underwriting results. Careful consideration should therefore be given to the need for and the value of size homogeneity before the decision is made to eliminate or do without a surplus treaty.

Relative cost is the second area of consideration. The method of determining the cost of an excess of loss contract at various retentions has been explained thoroughly in this chapter. If there is currently a treaty in force, the costs of it are known; so the two can be compared to see which is actually least expensive. Generally, if the net retention is set above the area of high loss frequency by utilizing one of the methods indicated earlier, the cost of the excess should be less than the cost of the surplus treaty.

Another consideration is the effect a larger net retention might have on the underwriter. There are two danger areas here. First, the underwriter, being a conservative person by nature who has been thinking in terms of the lower limits for years, will be stunned by the change. As a result, he probably will refuse to take a full line on good risks and refuse outright other risks which might have otherwise been accepted. If pushed by management, he might start accepting the full exposure on the surface. As soon as possible, however, he will reinsure a portion of it facultatively. "Too high a retention often leads to greater use of agency and facultative reinsurance than is desirable, and the company is generally unable to exercise control over this outlet."[13] This has been such a problem that a few companies have only been able to successfully overcome the difficulty on first conversion by not materially changing the underwriting procedure. They allow the underwriters to continue setting just about the same retention on the risks that they were previously setting under the treaty. The difference is that instead of actually reinsuring from that retention, someone else takes off the balance between the retention set by the underwriter and the net retention on the excess contract. This balance is placed in a separate, self-reinsurance account. Gradually, the retention under which the underwriter is working is raised until the full excess retention is finally reached.

Secondly, another danger as far as underwriters are concerned is that they will be affected in just the opposite manner as the above instance; i.e., they start "writing against" the excess. The underwriters, knowing that their maximum possible loss is definitely limited to their net retention, start accepting a larger share of the risks presented to them. They also start accepting liability on risks that they would have previously rejected. Because the underwriters are writing against the excess, the loss experience takes a big jump and the cost of keeping the net retention at the level previously established becomes prohibitive. A degree of control can be maintained over this situation by carefully watching the volume of premiums written prior to changing over to excess of loss reinsurance as compared with the volume written after the change. Spot audits and investigation of larger losses provide management sufficient control to limit this activity. If a serious amount of this practice is discovered, facultative cessions will reduce the exposure and bring the underwriting standards back into line before enough losses are incurred to seriously effect the rate of the excess of loss contract.

Another factor in the Treaty vs. Excess of Loss conflict is the question, "By utilizing a reinsurance program composed purely of excess of loss contracts, is the reinsurer standing on the same footing as the ceding company?" Is the reinsurer accepting equal liability for

[13]John C. Steggles, "Proper Utilization of Excess of Loss can benefit Insurer," *The Review,* XCIII, No. 4115 (December 7, 1962), p. 1429.

basically the same rate? The rates for excess of loss reinsurance are computed so that the reinsurer is almost assured of getting its money back within five years. If everything goes well, the reinsurer may also realize a substantial percentage loading which will more than meet its expenses and yield a profit.

The ceding company's rates, on the other hand, are set by filings it has made subject to the approval of the state boards of insurance. There is no guarantee that it is going to cover losses plus expenses, much less make a profit. If a treaty were used, the rate the reinsurer receives would be essentially the same rate the ceding company received from the policyholder; consequently, the two parties are sharing a mutual fortune. If the reinsurance commission is at the level of the insurer's cost, when the ceding company loses, the reinsurer loses as well. However, under excess of loss, when the ceding company makes a profit, the reinsurer makes a profit; but when the ceding company experiences a loss, the reinsurer may still make its profit. As a general rule, however, such a situation only develops when the primary insurer's underwriting weakens to the point where its loss ratio deteriorates due to high frequency and/or inadequate rates as a result of over aggressiveness. In this situation, it is only proper that the primary insurer should stand alone.

It would not be fair, however, to leave the subject without considering the other side of the argument. What about in the other instances when the ceding company is making a nice profit? The rate of profit for the reinsurer remains at a constant level, assuming a constant loading and constant cost, no matter how much the experience under the contract improves. At the same time, the ceding company's profit rises with the improving of experience. The ceding company is obviously considerably better off than the reinsurer in those circumstances.

The above considerations seem to indicate that during the period of falling profits and narrow profit margins, the primary insurer would be in a better position if it had a surplus treaty. Conversely, during a period of respectable profits with the trend toward better things to come, the primary insurer might be wise to switch to excess of loss coverage. The reverse of this has occurred in the past, reflecting the conflict of interests between the primary insurer and the reinsurer. As results have worsened, ceding companies have lost their pro-rata treaties and had no alternative but to switch to excess of loss coverage. The primary insurer has been required to sacrifice some reinsurance protection or pay a higher cost for its coverage at a time when it can least afford either alternative. The insurer is placed between the proverbial "rock and a hard spot." Its loss ratio is rising on one hand, and its reinsurance costs are rising on the other. Instead of easing the strain on the industry during the down side of the cycle, the reinsuring segment compounded the problem.

The purpose of this discussion is not to condemn the practices of professional reinsurers. Rather, the purpose is to bring into perspective the Treaty vs. Excess of Loss conflict. Reinsurers are naturally going to push the voluntary switch to Excess of Loss during times of slim profit margins. The primary insurer who accepts these overtures without serious consideration of the many facets involved may be acting contrary to the best interests of its shareholders.

CHAPTER SUMMARY

In order to accurately design a reinsurance program which brings value and reinsurance coverage received into agreement, the general reinsurance needs of the company should be outlined. The second phase is comparing the present program with the needs developed in the first phase. Often it will be discovered that the program has not been fulfilling these needs at all. In fact, on occasion, contracts have been discovered to be aggravating rather than helping the situation. A preliminary investigation should then be made to establish (1) what forms of reinsurance are best suited for satisfying the needs and (2) what other insurers are doing who face similar problems.

After the acceptable forms of reinsurance are established, the net retention should be set for the excess of loss contracts proposed. If a pro-rata treaty is desirable and/or necessary, its retentions should be set and enough lines established to ensure complete utilization of the treaty facilities during the normal course of operations. Any larger risks which exceed the treaty capacity would be handled either facultatitvely or through a facultative obligatory treaty.

If excess of loss reinsurance is utilized, the net retention must be set to allow the primary insurer to balance cost with value. On an exposed excess, the net retention should be placed so that the area of high loss frequency falls within the net retention. Three methods which effectively set the net retention are the Variation in Loss Ratio Method, the Loss Frequency Method, and the Integrated Cost Method. In setting the net retention for an unexposed excess, the maximum underwriting limit may be the standard used, or the Cushion Theory may be used. Consideration should be given as to whether to state the net retention as a flat or aggregating amount.

Once an acceptable reinsurance program is established, it must be periodically reviewed to ensure that it is still efficiently performing the functions it was originally designed to perform. The general reinsurance needs must also be periodically reviewed to ensure that the needs are still present and as active as when the program was established. Thus, in reinsurance programming, as with any other programming situation, the validity of the program developed remains so only as long as the needs remain the same. As a consequence, the program must remain as flexible as possible and be under continual review.

CHAPTER VI

Selection of Your Reinsurer

> Your reinsurance man should be your best friend. He is one of your ablest counselors and one of your best business doctors. He has at your disposal a vast store of technical information and training. He has facilities and capacities which can be tailored to almost any legitimate need.[1]

THIS QUOTE by J. H. Laidlaw reflects the extreme importance of the decisions surrounding the selection of a reinsurer. It emphasizes that not only is the primary insurer establishing a legally binding contract for protection and/or risk sharing, but it is also establishing a business relationship which may offer many fringe benefits. This chapter is included in order to give air to some of the many facets which might well be considered before the reinsurer is finally selected. The following discussion does not presuppose that an insurer, on its own initiative, contacts the reinsurer(s) it selects. Because of our free enterprise system in which competition and initiative are the rules, the insurer is constantly being presented with a vast array of reinsurance personalities and offers.

This chapter is presented in an endeavor to enable the reader to better assess the true functions of the reinsurer and those of the reinsurance broker who often enters into the negotiation of reinsurance agreements. As no discussion of reinsurance would be complete without consideration of the practice of reciprocity, a discussion of its advantages and disadvantages as a substitute for the professional reinsurer for pro-rata treaty reinsurance is included here to round out the consideration of reinsurers.

[1]J. H. Laidlaw, "What Does a Company Want From Its Reinsurance?" as reported in *Speaking of Reinsurance*, edited by George F. Rutledge.

EVALUATION OF THE REINSURER

In evaluating the relative strength and desirability of a prospective reinsurer, there appear to be five general areas of consideration, running the spectrum of categorical verbiage from financial condition to miscellaneous. Since the reinsurance agreement is first and foremost a financial one, the primary area of concern is the reinsurer's financial condition.

Financial Condition

Although the reinsurer is an important partner of the insurer during the normal course of operation, it is during the times of catastrophies, conflagrations, and calamities that the financial backing by the reinsurer is most needed. Therefore, consideration of the financial character is of utmost importance. The first standard in measuring the financial character of the reinsurer is its financial strength. Among the measures useful for such a comparison between reinsurers are (1) the ratio of earned premium income to surplus, (2) the ratio of paid up capital to earned premium income, (3) the amount of subscribed capital and the financial condition of the subscribers, and (4) the ratio of premium and capital reserves to earned premium income. These should be considered not only in the light of how much, but also in terms of quality and ability to pay large losses immediately. All of these factors are relative measures. An orderly comparison between the prospective reinsurers for each factor will disclose the relative strength of each.

Another important area of financial character is the loss payment reputation of the reinsurers. The only thing worse than a financially defective reinsurer is one who attempts to deny liability at the slightest provocation. Since the reinsurance agreement is between "informed" parties, there should be few, if any, areas of uncertainty. A reinsurer who is easily provoked into denying liability and delays decisions on every small deviation, is obviously not an "informed" party and is thus professionally incompetent. Reinsuring with a reinsurer of such a reputation would obviously be as much protection to the ceding company as cut-rate, no guarantee sprinklers against fire are to the commercial property owner.

Retrocession Policies and Retrocessionaires

The reinsurer uses the practice of retroceding a share of its liability accepted in order to increase its capacity. It would therefore be of use to temper the judgment of the financial condition of the reinsurers with the knowledge of their respective retrocession arrangements. The financially weaker reinsurer might retain, net, a smaller amount of liability and have more dependable retrocessionaires than a stronger reinsurer. As a result, the weaker reinsurer might actually be as financially secure as the stronger one. Knowledge of the retrocession arrangement in most cases is difficult to obtain. If, however, an insurer has access to such information, it should be taken into consideration when analyzing the reinsurer's financial strength.

Management

Another important area which enters in the making of an excellent reinsurer is the quality of management. Broad knowledge of the executives concerning not only the present reinsurance practices but also the problems and practices of primary insurers is a must. They must have sound answers or at least have a method which can be utilized in finding a satisfactory solution to the insurer's problems. If they are to be the primary insurer's "best friend, ablest counselors, and best business doctors," they must possess this broad knowledge and carry it with ease. Finally, they must be of unquestioned integrity.

Flexibility

The reinsurer must have sufficient facilities and capabilities to offer the required forms of reinsurance at competitive rates. It must not only be capable of meeting the needs of the ceding company, but it must also be willing to be flexible in the coverages desired in order to adequately satisfy those needs. A reinsurer who will offer only the standard coverages is of no great value to the ceding company in the long run.

Miscellaneous

Not to be overlooked are the miscellaneous advantages a good reinsurer can offer to its ceding companies. Special services offered to the young primary insurer can be invaluable in the establishment of a successful operation. Special services would include such items as advice concerning claims, underwriting, systems and procedures, licensing and regulatory problems, and rehabilitation.

THE PROFESSIONAL REINSURER VS. RECIPROCITY

Because of the need to meet competition in the areas of both price and services, many primary insurers have found reciprocity particularly attractive when treaty reinsurance is required. The golden promise of maintenance of premium volume and a large reduction in the net cost of reinsurance has lured many primary insurers into assuming the role of reinsurers themselves. Reciprocity is the practice of placing treaties on a reciprocal basis, one against another, so that a ceding company will only give a share of its treaty to a reinsurer who is able to offer another in return. The normal practice is for one insurer to require an equal share of another insurer's treaty covering the same type of policies, in consideration for a share of the offering insurer's treaty. Basically, this means that Insurer A offers Insurer B a one percent share, for example, of Insurer A's first surplus fire treaty only if Insurer B will reciprocate with an offer to Insurer A of a share of its first surplus fire treaty producing a comparable premium income or profit.

The normal requirements are, first, to require as close a matching or premiums ceded as possible so that neither insurer's gross premium volume will fluctuate to any degree. Secondly, the matching of premium volume should yield an equitable exchange of profits on the business ceded. If the profits realized on each share are not equal, an additional share of the deficient insurer's treaty is required so as to compensate the other insurer for the loss in profits.[2] Thus, the objectives of reciprocity come to light, (1) to maintain premium volume, (2) to increase the amount of profits realized in relation to invested capital, and (3) to reduce the net cost of reinsurance to the primary insurer to the lowest level possible – that of handling cost. With these objectives as a basis, it is now possible to discuss the relative advantages and disadvantages in the use of reciprocity.

Professional Reinsurer

A professional reinsurer may be defined as a reinsurer who depends upon the transaction of reinsurance business as its sole enterprise. For the purpose of this discussion, primary insurers who assume reinsurance without reciprocity may be considered as offering the advantages of the professional reinsurer with three reservations: (1) the insurer must be relatively large with a substantial premium volume on reinsurance assumed; (2) the insurer may be in competition with the reinsured, a disadvantage not present if the services of the professional reinsurer as defined above were utilized; and (3) because the acceptance of reinsurance is a secondary function of these insurers, the advantages of the use of the professional reinsurer will be present but normally not to so great a degree.

[2]There are many other factors which should be considered, even before the ones mentioned, however, these two are the two most commonly mentioned as requirements for reciprocity and are, therefore, necessary for an understanding of the practice. For a detailed analysis of the other factors operating in a reciprocal exchange, see Chapter VII, "The Art of Reciprocity," see page 147.

Advantages of the Professional Reinsurer. There are several advantages attributed to the use of the professional reinsurer as opposed to the use of reciprocity, not the least of which is the fact that the primary insurer is dealing with a professional whose sole business and interest is reinsurance. The reinsurer is technically competent (having to deal successfully with hundreds of ceding companies). Because its sole activity is the acceptance of reinsurance, the professional reinsurer offers greater flexibility and dealings in confidence.

The professional reinsurer must be flexible, for it has to meet the demands of the primary insurers in order to stay in business. This flexibility is further enhanced by the reinsurer's freedom from rigid state control. If a new form of reinsurance agreement is necessary to satisfy the needs of the ceding company, the reinsurer is not only required to offer it, but it also has the freedom to do so.

The ceding company, in dealing with the professional reinsurer, may do so in confidence, for it may be assured that nothing concerning the information which passes between the two of them will ever be disclosed to a competitor. Because the reinsurer must be familiar with many facets of the ceding company's operations, it may be exposed to information which might be of great value to the ceding company's competitors.

One of the necessary characteristics of reciprocity is that the insurer establishes many bilateral reinsurers. To have many reinsurers means to have many hours spent in costly negotiations and long-distance phone calls and a vastly enlarged reinsurance department with the attending high administrative costs. The professional reinsurer offers the answer to all of the above objections of reciprocity. He is delighted to handle all of the reinsurance arrangements of the primary insurer. This means that only one negotiation is necessary, time and expense is saved, and the reinsurance department can be reduced or maintained at the "half-a-girl" level.

In a growth situation, the primary insurer may be required to utilize the services of the professional reinsurer in order to obtain growth financing. Because the reinsurer has the responsibility of maintaining the unearned premium reserves on the business accepted, reciprocity is of no financing aid in such a situation. If the insurer succeeds in maintaining its premium volume through reciprocity, it will have to maintain the original amount of unearned premium reserve.

The final primary advantage of the use of the professional reinsurer as opposed to reciprocity is the often repeated phrase that "they will stand by you in good times or bad." This advantage for the professional reinsurer is the result of the misuse of reciprocity by many reciprocal reinsurers. One of the selling points of reciprocity is that an insurer can balance this bad experience in one area against the good experience of other insurers in other areas. In time, the other insurers will be balancing their bad experience against the insurer's good experience. All of the fluctuation is, of course, due to the cyclical trends in evidence in every aspect of the business world. However, some reciprocal reinsurers are plagued with short memories and can never remember when they were having bad experience and being supported, in part, by their reinsurers. As a consequence, as soon as a ceding company's treaty starts showing bad results, the treaty is cancelled, and the reinsurer withdraws its profitable treaty from the temporarily unfortunate ex-reciprocal reinsurer.

The hazard of reciprocal cancellation may not look so disastrous to a primary insurer upon first consideration. An insurer practicing reciprocity will have many reinsurers and can therefore easily make other arrangements. Unfortunately, this is not the case; as in periods of unprofitability of the treaty, many notices of cancellation may be received, some of them contingent and others of a final nature. The effect of these cancellations is the loss of costly efforts of negotiation and establishment of the exchanges, therefore requiring more expenditures when the insurer can least afford it – when it is having a bad run of business. In trying to find replacement reinsurers, many valuable concessions may have to be given in order to get reciprocity of like quality to that which was cancelled. As a result, the net cost of reinsurance is increased. The insurer may also find that even by offering concessions it is unable to attract the desired reciprocity. The only course left open to the insurer is to turn to reciprocal reinsurers who were likewise cancelled because of the poor results of their treaties. On the other hand, the professional reinsurer has to stick by its ceding companies as long as possible. The profits to be derived during good times will be from the same insurers whose treaties are presently showing a loss due to cyclical variations.

Disadvantages. The only disadvantage in the use of the professional reinsurer over reciprocity is in the passing of considerable profits on the part of the ceding company to the professional reinsurer. This is not the case with the use of reciprocity. This comes back to the question of the value of supporting another strata of insurers in the industry. For many years, the industry did without the aid of the professional reinsurer. It was not until the advent of the treaty that the professional reinsurer, as known today, came into being. Up to the coming of the treaty, all reinsurance was done facultatively and generally on a reciprocal basis. Thus, the question follows as to whether professional reinsurers are necessary now. The answer to this question seems to be yes, due to the need for financing growth by the younger companies, the mishandling of reciprocity by the primary insurers, the cost of establishing and maintaining international agreements in respect of smaller companies, and the need for excess of loss coverage which is presently not offered on a reciprocal basis.

The Use of Reciprocity

Whenever a period of good profits for the primary insurers occurs, the reinsurance pie offered through reciprocity looks tempting indeed. All the primary insurers see is the profits they are "unnecessarily" passing on to their reinsurers. Then, as the cycle swings the other direction and profits become slimmer and more elusive, the popularity of the practice falls off. What makes reciprocity a "fair weather" partner? A look at the advantages and disadvantages associated with reciprocity might furnish an idea as to the reasons behind its fluctuating popularity.

Advantages. Reciprocity enables the primary insurer to maintain its premium volume. If the shares of the treaties exchanged represent approximately the same premium income, each insurer will be able to maintain a volume of premiums almost equal to the direct premiums written. This would not be the case if a professional reinsurer were used. The premium volume, as well as the level of the unearned premium reserve, would be reduced by the amount of the cessions made to the professional reinsurer. The advantages which accrue from the high premium volume are: (1) the statistics will show a substantially higher premium volume; (2) the dollar amount of profits may be higher; (3) there will be more dollars to invest.

$1,000,000	Direct premium income
480,000	80% ceded for 40% reinsurance commission
$ 520,000	Net premium remaining to Company A
110,000	55% losses on remaining liability
$ 410,000	Balance after payment of losses
400,000	Acquisition and administration expenses
$ 10,000	PROFIT

The above example is included to illustrate the attraction of the increase in profits available to the primary insurer through the use of reciprocity. Company A's acquisition and administration expenses amount to forty percent of the premium income. The company has a quota share agreement with a professional reinsurer under which eighty percent of the liability is ceded for a reinsurance commission of forty percent. Premium income under the treaty for the past year was $1,000,000, the loss ratio being fifty-five percent. Company A realized a gross profit on the business retained of five percent.

If this had been a reciprocal arrangement, with a five percent average profit experienced on reinsurance assumed, and with an equal premium volume, the year's end profit statement would have looked like this:

$1,000,000	Direct premium income
480,000	80% ceded for reinsurance commission
$ 520,000	Direct net premium income
480,000	Reinsurance net premium income, after commission
$1,000,000	Net premium income
550,000	55% losses
$ 450,000	Balance after payment of losses
400,000	Acquisition and administration expenses
$ 50,000	PROFIT

Thus, although the profit realized remained constant, five percent, the dollar amount of profit increased by five hundred percent. Since investors measure the success of a company in the return on invested capital, if the amount of paid up capital and surplus in Company A is $500,000 representing 100,000 shares, the comparative results would look like this:

	PROFESSIONAL REINSURER	RECIPROCITY
I. Earnings as a percentage of paid up capital and surplus	2%	10%
II. Earnings per share	$0.10	$0.50

However, the ratio of liabilities to paid up capital and surplus would be less when reciprocity is used. Unearned premium reserve, a liability, remains at $1,000,000 under reciprocity, but is reduced to $200,000 when the professional reinsurer is used. If the ceding company, Company A, were able to safely remain at risk for its full premium writings and yet reduce its total commitment per risk to twenty percent of the value of each policy issued, it then can make a substantial increase in profits. Reciprocity allows the primary insurer to bring its premium income back to its original level without sacrificing reinsurance coverage.

Through reciprocity, the primary insurer is able to achieve a spread of risk that is available to him in no other way. This is one of the greatest selling points of reciprocity, one behind the reason for its use by many insurers, particularly those whose treaty upon which the reciprocity is based is world-wide. Recalling the example above, the effect of the spread obtained is obvious. Twenty reciprocal reinsurers assumed eighty percent of the direct business written by Company A. Each one assumed a four percent share and gave in return a four percent share of its quota share treaty. The maximum possible loss to any of the reinsurers for a $10,000 risk written by Company A would be $400. On the business assumed by Company A, under the same circumstances, the maximum possible loss would be $400. The commitment on any one risk has thus been reduced to manageable proportions, and a spread has been attained of twenty $400 risks in exchange for one $8,000 risk.[3] There are two primary advantages of attaining such a spread: (1) A large number of risks are insured, thereby allowing the Law of Large Numbers to work with relative efficiency; and (2) the maximum commitment on any one risk is kept to such a small level that the effects of accumulation and of a catastrophe in any one area will not have a noticeable effect upon the loss ratio.

The reduction of the net cost of reinsurance is another advantage assigned to the practice of reciprocity. Because the primary insurer is also acting the part of the reinsurer, the profits it passes on to the reinsurers are balanced, under ideal circumstances, by the profits being passed to it by its ceding companies. As a result, if the profits and premiums are successfully balanced, the primary insurer's net cost of reinsurance will be reduced to the costs of negotiating and administering the various treaties. Under these circumstances, this could accurately be called "reinsurance at cost."

Reciprocity gives the primary insurer a larger amount of investable capital than it would have if a professional reinsurer were used exclusively. This is obviously a collateral advantage of the maintenance of a high premium volume. Previously, the premiums had been ceded to the reinsurers, thus causing a loss to the ceding company of the amount of possible interest that could have been earned on the amount ceded. Through reciprocity, the reinsurance premiums re-

[3]An insurer who is utilizing reciprocity correctly, probably will have in excess of fifty reinsurers in order to reduce the shares even further, however, twenty was used for simplicity's sake.

ceived may be invested, thus allowing recovery of earnings that had been previously passed on to the reinsurer.

With the grave concern surrounding the balance of payments situation and the Senate investigations of the insurance industry, the volume of premium dollars leaving the United States to foreign reinsurers is of prime concern. By arranging equal reciprocity with foreign markets, the domestic market can continue to obtain foreign contracts and yet help ease a serious problem by matching these "invisible exports" with "invisible imports." With the industry going to such great lengths to avoid government intervention in insurance, the use of reciprocity for this purpose seems to be a rather painless way of avoiding the feared governmental action in this area.

One of the most incessant problems of the industry since World War II has been the lack of capacity. The capacity problem has become critical as a result of the tremendous increase in the size of industrial processes and the general inflation of values over the years since World War II. The restricted capacity of the U.S. market in certain areas has often resulted in business being passed to foreign insurers through the surplus lines market. With the wider utilization of reciprocity on the part of the primary insurers, the market capacity can be expanded almost overnight to many times its present size.

Disadvantages. Reflected throughout the previous discussions were the many disadvantages in the use of reciprocity. A primary disadvantage is that the insurers may find that they are reinsuring risks which they had declined, or would have declined, as direct business. A good example of this occurred in Euorpe in the late 1950's. At rates which later proved to be inadequate, French marine insurers insured foreign hulls far below rates being quoted in London, and they passed a large part of the liability back to London under their marine hull treaties at these inadequate rates. These were rates which the London underwriters had previously refused to meet on the very risks they were compelled to accept under the treaties. The end result was that the French passed a good share of the losses back to the London market. With London's kind assistance, the French managed to steal a great deal of business from them. This sort of thing can happen quickly. The hazard can be reduced to manageable proportions, however, by careful selection of reciprocal reinsurers and by ensuring that the underwriting policies and rates are in agreement between all parties concerned.

Wide spread usage of reciprocity might possibly eliminate a few professional reinsurers.

> Ought we not ask ourselves which we prefer, the immediate gain, if gain it be, which reciprocity brings to a direct office, or the ultimate good, which the existence of a strong professional reinsurance element in the insurance body public may bring.[4]

Because of the factors enumerated at the close of the section on professional reinsurers, it is doubted that the majority of them would have to close shop due to reciprocity. Several of our strongest professional reinsurers have their home offices abroad where they are doing well and where, incidentally, the practice of reciprocity is widespread. The professional reinsurer may exchange some of its business with the primary insurer, thereby maintaining its position if insurers were demanding reciprocity. It is obvious that the reinsurer does not have enough premium income to reciprocate on an equal share with most of its reinsureds, but it can do reasonably well in this area, if required, on a match of profits between the treaty assumed and the retrocession treaty.

By utilizing reciprocity, the insurer may not enjoy the professional advice it would receive from the professional reinsurer. As a professional in the area of reinsurance, the reinsurer can be depended upon to furnish sound, impartial service and advice. On the other hand, the reciprocal reinsurer may well be just another primary insurer with exactly the same problems the primary insurer has, with neither of them having the answer. If one insurer does have an answer, competition may require that it not be disclosed. Another problem of not dealing with the professionals is that the primary insurer is not assured that all transactions will be quickly and efficiently handled; the neophyte reinsurer may take exception, pay claims late and after much litigation, and not conform to market practices in general. It may not be trying to make things hard for everyone, but it simply is in unfamiliar waters.

The primary insurer who practices reciprocity may have difficulty in keeping reciprocal exchanges when business takes a turn for the worse. Invariably, no matter how carefully the portfolio of direct business is maintained, provisional notices of cancellation will be received. Someone is always unhappy. If the experience has been bad, unfavorable, or borderline, a number of provisional notices of cancellation will be received, probably sprinkled with a few definite notices of cancellation. This causes many anxious moments on the part of the primary insurer. The insurer has to face the hazard of possibly being committed on a risk without complete reinsurance coverage.

Reciprocity has the further disadvantage of tending to astronom-

[4] K. R. Thompson, *Reinsurance*, (Philadelphia: Chilton Company, 1951), p. 29.

ically increase the number of reinsurers, with a directly proportional increase in the costs of handling the reinsurance transactions. Further, when considering an offer of reciprocity, the insurer is under pressure to accept the offer even if its underwriting judgment says otherwise. The pressure is the result of the need to place a share of its own treaty.

The hazard of accumulation is far greater under reciprocity than if the primary insurer utilized the professional reinsurer. It can evaluate its accumulation of risks in its direct writings with relative ease, but the insurer has no way of knowing how many more risks it is insuring in the same area by way of reinsurance. This hazard is further aggravated in the fire lines through undisclosed risks by virtue of the Reinsuring or Operative Clause of the treaty which accepts within the scope of the treaty "all insurances, whether accepted direct or by way of reinsurance, against the risk of . . ." The "by the way of reinsurance" increases the hazard. When the underwriter is considering accepting a treaty, he has a fairly good idea of the area in which the company is writing directly. He does not know, however, what he will catch under this phrase, and he has no way of finding out.

Finally, reciprocity of an international character has the disadvantage of exposing the primary insurer to immediate cancellation (normally forty-eight hours) upon the outbreak of war. The cancellation means that the insurer will find itself with a large gap in its reinsurance coverage which may expose it to catastrophic losses before other arrangements can be made. If the primary insurer had, on the other hand, established reinsurance agreements with a professional or reciprocal reinsurer in the United States, this problem would not exist.

Because of the many possible disadvantages, an insurer who decides to utilize reciprocity should tread with caution. Probably, many of the disadvantages listed above are due to the lack of adequate preparation on the part of the participants. This would indicate that if operated properly, the practice could offer an area of increased return to the insurer. One of the best places to obtain experienced and independent advice as to the applicability and practices of reciprocity, and reinsurance generally for that matter, is from a competent reinsurance broker.

THE REINSURANCE BROKER

The purpose of the reinsurance broker is to place at the disposal of the primary insurer a world of reinsurers and ceding companies, wide market knowledge, and impartial, experienced counsel. The common functions of reinsurance intermediaries and the advantages and disadvantages associated with their use are considered in this section.

The broker is an indispensable link in the chain of international reinsurance operations. Outside the United States, the primary insurers deal with the intermediaries rather than directly with other insurers and reinsurers. The broker is normally of international character, having ties in the major insurance markets in this country and abroad. He is therefore able to relieve his clients from the need of developing costly international ties in order to effect the desired reinsurance arrangements. Because of his international character, the broker is well informed on the practices of the major insurance markets, plus other information such as the past loss experience in any particular area, the strong companies in the market, the most attractive treaties available, and the major catastrophe hazards present. He is familiar with the standard reinsurance practices between countries and can therefore ensure that his client is getting the best or standard agreement in the market.

If the primary insurer is practicing reciprocity, the broker offers the attractive service of being able to deal with all of its reciprocal reinsurers. The insurer is thus able to maintain the same sized reinsurance department it would have under a professional reinsurer. Only one statement of treaty cessions made is required by the insurer, and it will receive one statement, if so desired, from the broker reflecting the net results of its reinsurance assumptions. In other words, the broker offers to the primary insurer a fully developed, highly professional "reinsurance department." It relieves the primary insurer of the costs of developing such a department which, for many primary insurers, would be economically prohibitive.

The broker is equipped to handle all negotiations between the parties, thus reducing the amount of negotiation expenses due to long-distance telephone calls, letters, and trips by executives which might otherwise be necessary. If reciprocity is required, he has a vast array of other clients with whom appropriate reciprocal exchanges can be made. The other technical services the broker offers to the primary insurer are the preparation, duplication, and distribution of the treaty or contract wording, analysis of the statements of account which are received from the other parties to ensure compliance with the agreement, and other details which arise under the agreements.

The broker offers the above services at a relatively low cost. The brokerage ranges normally from one to five percent of the earned premiums ceded under the treaty and ten percent of the premium of an excess of loss contract. The wide difference in percentage between treaty and excess brokerage is because the broker has minimum expenses which are incurred in the negotiation of an agreement. Since the premium under the excess of loss form is smaller than the treaty form, the rate has to be higher, but the resulting dollar charge is normally less. This percentage charge is paid by the reinsurer to the broker for acquiring the business.

There is a point where the cost of the broker exceeds the cost which would be incurred if the primary insurer handled all of its own reinsurance arrangements. The primary insurer should cease using the broker when the premium volume ceded under the treaty attains such magnitude that the brokerage charge exceeds the costs to the primary insurer of setting up its own facilities and handling its own negotiations. However, to the vast number of insurers, the services offered by the broker are being purchased at a far smaller cost than they could be developed and maintained by the individual insurer, unless reinsurance is placed directly with one or two professional reinsurers.

Needless to say, the broker offers complete independence, if such is possible. Part of this independence is the anonymity which is given to the primary insurer by the broker. He can put out "feelers" and ask for offers without directly involving his client. If the primary insurer does not like the offer received, it can request that the negotiations go no further as far as the particular insurer is concerned, and no feelings are hurt or business associations ruined.

As can be expected, the use of the reinsurance broker is not all sunlight and flowers. The cost is relatively small for the benefits received only if the primary insurer is striving (1) for a number of reinsurers, part or all of whom are in other markets and/or (2) for reciprocity. In the United States, one cannot expect the reinsurer to absorb all of the cost of brokerage and give reinsurance coverage at the same price it could be obtained if there were no brokerage to pay. Some professional reinsurers in the United States refuse to recognize the broker with this in mind. In addition, they actively provide services which the broker does not generally provide. The controlling motives of the reinsurance underwriter is the balance of profits between premiums and losses. The reinsurance intermediary's livelihood is completely dependent upon commissions. As such, the intermediary's primary service is to provide indemnity at minimum cost. He is a marketing specialist. Services other than marketing dissipate commission income for purposes in which they have no direct financial interest. The professional reinsurer, on the other hand, has a selfish interest in providing services to its customers — underwriting, claims, accounting, statistical, rehabilitation, etc. to the extent that they may improve the customer's underwriting results and hence its own. In the areas the primary insurer requires these services, the direct contact will prove quite valuable. The broker here adds one step in the negotiations between a literate buyer and a literate seller and brings about an arms-length contractual relationship rather than a business marriage.

Choosing Your Broker

If the reinsurance broker is to perform the functions discussed in this section, he has to be running an efficient organization. Although it would be nice to report that all reinsurance brokers are of outstanding character and financially responsible, such is not the case. Since a considerable amount of material and money must be handled by the broker, it is of utmost importance that he be chosen with care and periodically subjected to a dispassionate appraisal.

In order to offer any truly valuable service to the primary insurer, he must have good international ties. This requirement is not satisfied by his claims to be "associated with John Doe, Ltd., Brokers at Lloyd's." Anybody can write to a Lloyd's broker and eventually get some sort of insurance coverage. Not only must the broker have international ties, he also must be well thought of and trusted by his contacts in those markets. Only in this way will he able to get the best coverage possible for his clients.

The reinsurance broker must be financially responsible to the point of being beyond reproach and of highest integrity. Checks for payment of premiums, claims, and any remittances are paid to the broker. He then pays the appropriate firms. Considerable sums of money are entrusted to him each month, and there are many temptations to the man who handles large sums of currency.

The broker should only be used when more than a few reinsurers are required. The primary insurer should arrange to pay a visit to the broker's offices to ensure that he has the staff and facilities necessary to efficiently handle the services to be required. The visit will also disclose whether he has sufficient background and flexibility to completely satisfy the insurer's needs. If the broker is offering the primary insurer the best in terms of a "reinsurance department," then he must have the facilities to do just that.

These are just a few of many things that should be considered when selecting a broker. If the broker being considered cannot satisfy all of the requirements, meet all of the descriptive characteristics, and offer all of the functions included in this section, pass on to the next broker on the list. There are many brokers who can more than meet these few requirements.

CHAPTER SUMMARY

The reinsurer, if properly chosen, can be a valuable aid to the primary insurer. Depending upon the objectives of the primary insurer, either the professional reinsurer, reciprocal reinsurers, or both may offer the best solution to the general needs of the firm. In evaluating the prospective reinsurer, professional or reciprocal, the following factors should be considered: (1) the financial condition, (2) retrocession policies and retrocessionaires, (3) the management, and (4) flexibility of services offered. Another area of consideration in choosing a treaty reinsurer is whether to use a professional reinsurer or reciprocity. The advantages of using the professional reinsurer are, (1) dealing with a professional, (2) dealings are confidential, (3) greater flexibility of services, (4) all of the reinsurance negotiations are handled at once, and (5) peripheral services not offered by the broker. The primary disadvantage attributed to the use of the professional reinsurer is the passing of profits to the reinsurer that could be avoided by utilizing reciprocity.

Reciprocity, on the other hand, offers the following advantages to those primary insurers willing to act as reinsurers: (1) high premium volume, (2) greater profits, (3) wide spread of risk, (4) reduction in the net cost of reinsurance, (5) more investable capital, and (6) automatically increasing the capacity of the market. There are, however, dangers which should be recognized before reciprocity is attempted; they can be summarized as follows: (1) cancellation of reciprocal agreements during times of poor experience, (2) assumption of risks at inadequate rates, (3) the position of the professional reinsurer being jeopardized, (4) not dealing with professionals, (5) increasing the indirect costs of reinsurance, (6) increasing the hazard of accumulation, and (7) exposing the primary insurer to unnecessary cancellation in the event of war.

The reinsurance intermediary plays an important role in the reinsurance picture. For a relatively low cost, he offers expert service, international ties, and reinsuring independence to the primary insurer. However, an insurer must use extreme caution in choosing the broker. In order to give the service required, he must be well versed in international reinsurance and be of highest integrity.

CHAPTER VII

The Art of Reciprocity

THESE ARE DAYS of increasing state supervision where rate regulation and price-cutting competition have created a rate structure in which the possibility of making an underwriting profit has almost vanished. It has become important to survival that the insurer continually search for ways to increase its return on invested capital. This search has led to such practices as the insurance agent also selling mutual fund shares, to the revision of investment policies, to devices for reducing the size of losses such as rehabilitation, and to the growing practice of reciprocity. There are many ways to reduce cost and improve underwriting experience, and both of these characteristics have been attributed to reciprocity. Thus, a thorough investigation of the way reciprocity is successfully practiced seems of particular value.

With any activity, there is a right way and a wrong way to accomplish the task. The practice of reciprocity is no exception. Much of the black that has been painted around this practice is not due to the lack of sound theory behind it or because it will not work, but rather because many of the participants jump into it with the idea of easy profits and only half-baked ideas as to how to carry on the business of reinsurance. This is why they pass out a multitude of notices of cancellation at the instant a small drop in the treaty profits is experienced. They do not utilize proper reinsurance underwriting due to their lack of proper investigation into just exactly how and why reciprocity is practiced. As a consequence, they find themselves holding the bag when the season's first hurricanes or similar catastrophes roll around. Because of these things, a stigma has become attached to both the word and practice of reciprocity in the United States.

This chapter has been developed in order to give recognition to reciprocity as a sound insurance practice. Insurers today must not overlook any area of possible cost reduction, and many are passing over reciprocity due simply to unfamiliarity with its techniques. This chapter contains the information necessary for sound consideration of the subject and its practice. Included in this chapter are some prerequisites before reciprocity should be considered, a brief look at some of the aspects of the role of the reinsurer, and some of the more important procedures to be followed in order to develop a reciprocal portfolio.

A GENERAL THEORY

Reciprocity is the practice of exchanging reinsurance contracts between primary insurers. Reciprocity is an excellent vehicle for the spread of risk between members of the insurance community. The average size of an insurer's maximum possible loss is reduced to the point where the consequences of accumulation and catastrophies are spread among the participating insurers with relatively little concentration in any one insurer. The primary insurer is able to enjoy reinsurance coverage and yet maintain a relatively high level of premium income. In order to attain these results, careful planning and coordinating is necessary as well as a thorough knowledge of the many ramifications of reinsurance and its practice. The first in a series of decisions the insurer will have to make in order to realize good results through reciprocity is that of settling upon a book of direct business which can be easily adapted to a reciprocal exchange.

SOME PREREQUISITES

The measure of success the primary insurer attains in its reciprocal efforts will be partially determined by the care with which the direct business to be covered is chosen. Not every line of insurance is conducive to reinsure reciprocally. Among other things, this choice will determine how large the market for reciprocity is, how simple or complex the negotiations will be, and how satisfactory will be the experience under the exchange.

The standard practices associated with the line of business chosen must be well recognized in the class of direct business selected. This assures the primary insurer that any requirements during treaty negotiations which are dictated by the practices surrounding the class of business will be well understood. Familiarity with the direct business not only shortens a potentially long and costly negotiation, but it also lends itself to the smooth functioning of the treaty. For example, certain unusual expenses may be incurred in the settling of a claim, or a peculiar method of claim settlements may be used on the part of the ceding company. If these are standard practices in the area for that line of business, they will not be questioned, but rather taken as the normal method of operation.

The necessity of wide recognition is particularly valid if international reciprocity is contemplated. Not only the practices of the primary insurer should be well known, but the practices surrounding the same line of business in the other countries where reciprocal reinsurers to be selected must also be widely recognized. This is further compounded by the various languages involved. Misunderstandings often can be due to the inability of either party to make himself understood on some minor technical point which might not have arisen had the practice been understood.

The basic policy to be covered by the treaty must be relatively simple, preferably composed of coverage of one or a few hazards. The possibility of misunderstandings arising because of the reciprocal reinsurers being uncertain as to exactly which hazards are covered and which are excluded by the policy, is increased as the number of hazards insured increases. The predictability of the experience under the treaty decreases with the number of hazards included under one policy, thus yielding it less attractive to prospective reinsurers. The hazards covered under the respective treaties to be exchanged should be as nearly identical as possible. The probability of finding a sufficient number of reciprocal reinsurers under a complicated, or unique coverage, is rather slim.

For best results in obtaining satisfactory reciprocal agreements, the treaty to be used for reciprocity must be of a nature to yield relatively stable experience. This added predictability enables the reinsurers to accurately assess the risks involved. It also reduces the number of cancellations which will be received as a result of poor experience or a sudden drop in profits.

It must be realized that reciprocity is by definition a two-way street. The requirements which are met by Company A's treaty, such as stability of experience, must also be a characteristic of the treaties accepted by way of reciprocity by Company A. The primary insurer is not giving away its best business; rather it is obtaining a better spread, thereby improving its experience on the better business. Instead of passing on to the professional reinsurer the above average, the average, and the below average business (although it too must be profitable in the long run), the premiums are being retained on the above average business through reciprocity. In those lines where the experience is unpredictable or rather poor, the premiums are unilaterally ceded to the reinsurer. This is an important point. Just as the surplus treaty is properly utilized to give size homogeneity to the class of business covered, reciprocity is the management tool properly utilized to give line homogeneity to the company. An insurer achieves line homogeneity in its insurance portfolio by passing to the reinsurer a larger portion of the liability on risks in lines characterized by high risk and low predictability of experience and retaining a larger portion of the liability, either net or through reciprocity, on those lines of low risk and high predictability of experience. The net result of this varying retention is the maximizing of profits and stabilization of experience. Normally, because of the wide spread of risk obtained through the use of reciprocity, better results are obtained than through retaining larger and larger portions of the direct business. The primary insurer can increase its retention in the good lines through reciprocity instead of through retaining greater amounts of the risks it directly insures. It will thereby improve its experience while it is improving its net premium income and net profit position. A greater spread of risk is the main ingredient.

The concept of line homogeneity is that highly volatile lines of business should be unilaterally reinsured and stable lines reciprocally reinsured. Particularly applicable to this rule is the area of general third party liability risks. This line should be unilaterally reinsured because of: (1) the wide fluctuation in experience, (2) the wide variations between the states' financial responsibility laws and in amounts of recovery, and (3) the time lag between the time of loss and settlement. This hazard is better covered with excess of loss reinsurance on a unilateral basis rather than treaty reinsurance on a reciprocal basis.

Also to be considered before accepting reinsurance is the company charter. Obviously, it must grant the insurer the ability to accept risks by way of reinsurance before reciprocal exchanges can be legally made. If the charter does not include such a provision, the problems involved in obtaining an amendment are normally insignificant.

THE ROLE OF THE REINSURER, GENERALLY

The primary insurer who assumes the role of a reinsurer through reciprocal exchanges should be familiar with the manner in which the successful reinsurer conducts its operations. As in direct insurance, the reinsurer must follow certain broad principles. These broad principles may be classified as: (1) distribution of business by class, (2) distribution of business by geographical area, and (3) methods of the ceding company.

When constructing its portfolio of business, the reinsurer must pay particular attention to attaining a balance between the various classes of business covered under various treaties. The various hazards insured present to the primary insurer different loss characteristics under both normal and unusual circumstances. A balance in the portfolio must be attained to allow the maximum compensating effect between the various lines. Another factor playing a strong role in requiring a balanced portfolio is that the ceding company retains a large portion of the highly predictable business and cedes to the reinsurer the business in which a large fluctuation in experience is expected. The reinsurer desires to obtain a balance between the various lines of business in an effort to reduce the aggregate fluctuation in experience of the entire portfolio. The reciprocal insurer does not need to be concerned with this principle as it selects the more profitable lines for reciprocity.

The second guiding principle to which a reinsurer must adhere is the securing of a wide geographical distribution of business accepted. A wide geographical spread is necessary for the maximizing of profits by the reinsurer. It allows for the maximum compensation between the fluctuations of experience between the various areas from which business is derived. Just as not all of the *lines* of business accepted by the reinsurer will be unprofitable at any one time, neither will all the *areas* in which the reinsurer has accepted treaties be unprofitable at any one time. This is the guiding principle behind the international character of reinsurance.

Reinsurance is most successfully conducted by obtaining as wide a spread as possible between countries, rather than restricting reinsuring activities to any one country or general geographical area. A reinsurer can expect to balance its earthqauke losses in California with the profits being realized on the treaties covering the earthquake hazard in Japan. The windstorm losses in the Texas area may not be offset by the profits on the extended coverage business in the East Coast areas; whereas, the chances are that this will hold true in most every instance between Texas and Japan. The wider the geographical spread, the less chance there is for heavy losses to be experienced in the majority of areas in which reinsurance is accepted.

When the reinsurer accepts a treaty, it has no control over the quality of the business ceded under the treaty, nor over the area from which it is secured, except as generally outlined in the treaty wording. The reinsurer no longer has the power to regulate its acceptances which it had under the strict use of facultative reinsurance. As a consequence, the reinsurer has shifted from risk underwriting to "company" underwriting. Company underwriting is accomplished by the underwriting of the primary management, its underwriting policies, and general quality of business to be ceded under the proposed treaty. Only in this manner can the reinsurer even approach an accurate underwriting situation.

THE TECHNIQUE OF CONTROLLED RECIPROCITY

The business of the reciprocal approach to reinsurance is one which is to be entered with caution and only if certain techniques are followed. Reciprocity must be controlled rather than hap-hazard. Since reciprocity is a modified version of reinsuring, certain methods of the professional reinsurer can be bypassed without a danger of adverse experience. Of the three principles discussed in the preceding section – distribution by line, distribution geographically, and the methods of the ceding company – only the distribution by line has no applicability to the reciprocal reinsurer. Obviously, distribution by line is attained on the direct portfolio; however, because of the few lines selected for reciprocity, line distribution cannot be obtained, nor is it in agreement with the objectives of the primary insurer. Only the most desirable lines are to be covered by reciprocal reinsurance. They do not require offsetting by other lines.

Geographical Spread

The importance of obtaining a wide geographical spread has been emphasized earlier. At the risk of being too repetitive, this is included again to add continuity to the total area of the techniques of controlled reciprocity. This principle is well expressed by Kenneth Thompson when he wrote:

> The fundamental principle of spreading and pooling risks as widely as possible should guide all countries in developing the international aspect of reinsurance. Reinsurance furnishes the only solid method by which major catastrophies can be absorbed by several countries. Its results should not be judged by a short experience, because a period of years is required to show its merits.[1]

There are some problems which appear with international reinsuring which are not incurred when the activities are limited to a sin-

[1]K. R. Thompson, *Reinsurance*, (Philadelphia: Chilton Co., 1951), p. 292.

gle nation. One of the first of these is the requirement by many states or nations that any insurer or reinsurer doing business within its boundaries be licensed by that state or nation. In the United States, some states require the reinsurer to be licensed in that state. If a primary insurer chooses to utilize the services of a non-admitted reinsurer, it is not relieved of maintaining the premium reserves which would be the case had an admitted reinsurer been used. In other states, there are no such requirements. In order to ensure compliance, the legal requirements must be checked prior to entry into any area.

There is another problem which interferes with the free working of the theory of wide geographical distribution. This is the problem of the freedom of exchange as effected by the variation in the value of the currency in the international exchange. Freedom of exchange is also effected by certain state requirements which do not allow ready transfer of its currency to other nations. Some other general considerations which enter into a firm's decision to transact business in a foreign state are economic stability, general political situation, and possible social unrest. These factors should be carefully evaluated prior to internationalization.

Small Shares

One of the most vital techniques to sound reciprocity is that of dividing the treaty to be used as the vehicle for reciprocity into many small shares. The normal method of dividing the treaty is by offering each prospective reciprocal reinsurer a percentage of one hundred percent of the treaty.

Shares offered under this system often range from as large as five percent on small treaties to as small as 0.1 percent on large treaties. As a general rule, the smaller the shares, the greater the spread and the smaller will be the effects of accumulation and catastrophes. There are two general rules to follow in splitting up a treaty: (1) the shares should not be so many that the indirect costs exceed the value received; and (2) the smallest share should not yield less than $15,000 estimated annual premium income.

The logic of the first rule, that the shares should not be so many that the indirect costs exceed the value received, becomes obvious when the following points are considered. If a reciprocal treaty has been divided into equal shares of 0.25 percent interest, there will have to have been four hundred separate negotiations. Negotiations are expensive, both in terms of dollars spent in telephone calls and letters and in terms of executive hours. Add to this the cost of writing and reproducing four hundred treaty wordings, and the costs become even higher. This is only the beginning. Every month four hundred individual statements of account will have to be prepared and sent out with remittances for the previous month's balance. Every month, four hundred individual statements of account will be received and will have to be carefully checked to insure that the terms of the agreements have been followed. All in all, for a year's business this breaks down into: four hundred separate negotiations; four hundred slightly different treaty wordings; 4,800 monthly statements of account sent to reinsurers; 4,800 monthly statements of account from reinsurers received and analyzed; and at least four hundred cumulative annual statements of account sent and four hundred received each year. These figures do not include those reinsurers who are also going to want quarterly and semi-annual statements as well. Unless the premium volume is so substantial that the above costs will be insignificant in comparison, such small shares should not be utilized.

The second rule takes the cost aspect into consideration by requiring that the smallest share should not yield less than $15,000 estimated annual premium income. Generally, it has been found that the costs associated with the negotiation and administration of a reciprocal treaty lose their significance and exceed the probable profit to be made when the treaty is divided into shares producing a premium income less than $15,000.

It is difficult to immediately set up a full treaty on a reciprocal basis with enough shares to allow for a good spread. The normal procedure is to start off rather slowly and gradually build up to full reciprocity. In this way, the primary insurer has time to develop its own methods and solidify its reinsurance underwriting procedures on a sound basis before the full commitment is realized.

Another side to this evolution requires consideration. How willing is the professional reinsurer to be used as the hand-rail, so to speak, for the primary insurer to lean upon for support while slowly entering into the depths of the reinsurance business on a reciprocal basis? Although the professional reinsurers will definitely not like this situation, they can be persuaded to perform the service for a number of reasons, competition being one. Only certain lines will be reciprocally reinsured, and the others will remain with some professional reinsurer. The professional reinsurer may also be promised that a minimum percent interest of the treaty will remain with it on a unilateral basis. Further, it is a fact that the primary insurer naturally "grows" into larger retentions under its existing treaties on its direct business. Reciprocity is simply a way to effect this growth in the retention and obtain a greater spread at the same time.

This latter point bears some amplification. One of the most popular doctrines of primary insurers and reinsurers alike is that the primary insurer should assume as much liability as possible since its business is risk assumption. As the ceding company grows, the retentions under its treaties should be increased, for the company is now financially able to assume greater liability. This is a fine concept if the primary insurer desires to sacrifice a degree of size homogeneity in those lines where it is required for maximum underwriting profit. Obviously, the primary insurer desires to maintain size homogeneity if at all possible. Even better results can be obtained through reciprocity, for not only is size homogeneity not sacrificed, but the insurer realizes far greater spread of risk than it initially had.

Thus, the professional reinsurer should not object to the utilization of reciprocity in order to increase the amount at risk per premium dollar. It is in the best interests of the primary insurer. If objections are made, they should be in the form of objections to the procedure being used to develop the reciprocity or to the reinsurance underwriting standards established by the primary insurer. The objections should not be of reciprocity *per se*. In other words, these objections should be those designed to help in the establishment of sound reciprocity and against the development of unsound reciprocity.

Treaty Balance. The balance of a treaty is determined by the ratio of the estimated premium income to maximum possible loss for each share under the treaty.[2] A primary insurer should not even consider reciprocity unless this ratio is at least one. One of the reinsurance underwriting yardsticks is that if the ratio is less than one, the reinsurer can expect to lose money on the treaty in the long run. For a younger company with a small premium volume, this ratio can be expected to be close to 1.0. The more mature a company is, however, the better balanced the treaty should be. If this is not the case, then there is some question about the underwriting policies in force, and the offer for an exchange is probably best refused. Generally, an ideally balanced treaty in the property-liability area is twenty to one, whereas in the marine area, ten to one is a good standard.

To illustrate how the balance of a treaty should improve as the premium volume grows, a few characteristics of the insurance business have to be taken into consideration. No matter what size the carrier, all primary insurers in the same line compete for the same business (with a few exceptions such as large commercial risks). Thus, for both the small insurer and the larger one, the average size of the risks insured are going to be approximately the same. The vari-

[2]See Chapter V, page 108.

ations in size of the average risk insured between the two insurers will be due to primarily two factors. The smaller insurer will have fewer risks insured, thus allowing an exceptionally small or exceptionally large risk to have a disproportionate effect on the average size of risks insured. Secondly, the larger company will have a larger number of high value risks insured which will raise the average value some, but the larger volume of smaller risks will keep this effect to a minimum. As a result of the relatively stable average size of risks insured, the balance of the insurer's treaty will continually improve as its premium volume grows. One variable in the formula remains relatively constant, maximum possible loss, and the premium income grows.

The primary insurer when considering a reciprocal exchange should try to balance the profitability of the two shares to be exchanged. Ideally, the limits of liability, the balance of the shares offered, and the profitability over the last five years should be equal. Obviously, it is going to be difficult, if not impossible, to match all of these factors; however, equitability requires that they be matched as closely as possible.

The limits of liability in the two shares to be exchanged should be approximately equal. The insurer should not accept a larger liability than is ceded for approximately the same premium. If this were the case, it would mean that a larger liability is being accepted by way of reinsurance than would be accepted, for the same premium, directly when the risk can be carefully underwritten. This brings out the danger of the primary insurer using only one measure for accepting reciprocity, that of premium volume. If the only consideration is maintenance of premium volume, the insurer may find itself assuming liability at inadequate premiums.

It can be well argued that if the last five years' profits match, even though the limits of liability may not match, the net result has been the same; and therefore, the exchange is basically sound. This could possibly result from Company A, whose liability ceded per share is $5,000, having less restrictive underwriting policies than Company B, whose liability ceded per share is $7,000. However, the weakness is that catastrophies and conflagrations make no distinction between the good risk and the bad one. They absorb both with the same dexterity. Consequently, if Company A exchanged shares with Company B on this basis, Company A would fare far worse at the hands of a catastrophe per premium dollar received through reinsurance than would Company B. By taking into consideration the balances of the respective shares offered, the parties can determine just exactly how much liability they are assuming per premium dollar. In this way, they can accurately eliminate the above dangers.

None of these measures can be used to the exclusion of the other two; nor can just two of these be used to the exclusion of the third. This has been already shown as concerns the exclusive use of any one and also as concerns the use of liability ceded and past profitability. However, can the liability and balance be utilized to the exclusion of past experience? The answer is no, for these two factors only match quantity. Past experience is a measure of the quality of risks ceded which has a great effect on the profits realized on a book of business. May past experience and balance be considered to the exclusion of the liability per share? This factor comes closer to being one which can be excluded because liability is being considered when the balance of the treaty is determined. However, if the limits of liability were not taken into consideration, the chances of the aggregation of losses as a result of a catastrophe are greater than they would be if the liabilities matched. The probability of finding an exact match between profit and balance is small. Thus, the decision as to whether the exchange is equitable can be better judged by considering the third factor, liability. For example, profitability matches, but Company A's treaty balance is twenty to one (estimated premium income to MPL), whereas Company B's treaty balance is fifteen to one. If the liability for a share of Company B's treaty is $500 as compared to Company A's $700, then the exchange might be equitable. If the reverse is true, however, the exchange should not be considered at all. Not only would Company A be accepting a greater liability for a smaller premium volume, but the chances of heavy losses due to abnormal losses is greater under Company B's treaty than under Company A's.

Matching of Original Policies

When practicing reciprocity, the primary insurer selects the best line of business so as to increase both its aggregate amount at risk and its spread in this line. For best results, the lines which yield less desirable results are unilaterally reinsured. In order to attain line homogeneity of the over all portfolio, the primary insurer reciprocally reinsuring should only accept exchanges where the original hazards insured are of the same nature as the ones ceded. The original policies covered by the treaty should be of like coverage. Ideally, they should be compared clause for clause in order to determine if the risk is covered to the same extent. In practice, however, it is common to request only the terms, conditions, exclusions, and extensions of the original policy concerned.

As the insurer is considering areas for possible exchanges, those with a greater catastrophe hazard should be avoided if possible. If for some reason the attraction of a particular area with a greater catastrophe hazard is greater than the resistance of this underwriting consideration, the hazard can be eliminated by specifically excluding it in the treaty wording. In such an instance, the other insurer normally warrants that it will not cede such hazards under the treaty. In the event one is ceded, the reinsurer will be informed so as to allow it to be specially handled by the reinsurer under its excess of loss contract or facultatively. The excess of loss method would be for it to be declared by the reinsurer to its excess of loss reinsurers as coming under their contract. The facultative method would be for the reinsurer to facultatively retrocede the entire risk or some portion thereof.

Matching of Treaty Wording

The treaty wording received should contain the same general provisions as the one given. Among the things to be checked would be the following: (1) exclusions to ensure that they match; (2) commencement and expiry of liability to ensure that business is ceded under the two treaties on the same basis; (3) determination of premiums; (4) commission and profit commission; (5) reserves and interest on reserves; (6) reciprocal cancellation; (7) war cancellation clause; and (8) arbitration clause.

Accumulation

The accumulation hazard plays an important role in the desirability of a treaty exchange. Accumulation is the hazard to the reinsuring company that it will exceed its normal limit of liability on any one risk or in any one area through reinsurance assumed. Accumulation is more common in the excess of loss area because it is by nature intended to be a conflagration/catastrophe cover. This hazard is present, however, in treaty reinsurance. The accumulation hazard is introduced into treaty reinsurance because of the lack of individual risk underwriting by the reinsurer and by elimination of detailed borderaux.

As a result of the accumulation hazards, reinsurers find that they receive claim advices from several ceding companies on the same loss. A good example of this is a triple marine collision of December 14, 1960, in the Bosphorus. Some London marine insurers each exceeded their retention several times over and had to pass the balance on to their excess of loss reinsurers, who in turn received many individual claims from this one loss. This is a hazard which reciprocity introduces and must be closely controlled.

There are basically three ways to handle the accumulation hazard. First, the effects of accumulation are considerably reduced by accepting small shares of each treaty offered. Secondly, the hazard may be reduced by accepting shares of treaties under which the direct business ceded is derived from different geographical areas. This does not completely eliminate the hazard, for two of the companies reinsured may have reciprocal arrangements with each other.

The final method of controlling accumulation is to actually make an effort to determine the possible amount of accumulation. This is a rather difficult maneuver; however, if it can be done, a considerable amount of the hazard can be eliminated. There are two ways to underwrite the accumulation hazard. First, the insurer should determine the approximate premium volume each reciprocal reinsurer cedes to it from specified geograhical areas. A schedule can then be drawn up displaying the company's aggregate premium volume derived from each area, both through direct writings and assumed through reinsurance. Maximum limits should be established for each area, and if a prospective reciprocal reinsurer's premium ceded will cause one of these limits to be exceeded, careful consideration should be given to this fact before the exchange is accepted.

If within the scope of the treaties to be exchanged risks are accepted "by way of other treaty reinsurances," another method of underwriting the accumulation hazard may be used. A list of treaty ceding companies with the appropriate maximum possible loss per company should be obtained from the prospective reciprocal reinsurer. This list should be compared to the insurer's list of ceding companies to determine if any ceding companies are on both lists, and if so, to what extent. If the combined commitment is not too great, the exchange can be made without the fear of the accumulation on any one loss exceeding a reasonable level. If, however, there are several ceding companies which are on both lists, the possibilities of both companies becoming heavily involved in a catastrophe or conflagration becomes a real hazard.

For example, an exchange is proposed between Company A and Company B for one percent interest each. The lists of respective ceding companies for each with the MPL is reproduced below.

COMPANY A		COMPANY B	
COMPANY	MPL	COMPANY	MPL
C	$4,000	I	$5,000
D	4,500	J	6,000
E	6,000	E	4,500
F	4,000	K	4,000
G	5,500	L	5,500
H	7,000	M	7,000

An investigation of the lists reveals that both companies are reinsurers on the same treaty for Company E. Assuming the maximum possible loss is realized by Company E and that Companies A and B had agreed on a one percent exchange, the results would be that Company A's aggregate loss would be $5,985, and Company B's aggregate loss would be $4,515. The effect is the same as if the risk had not been reinsured by A and B. Because of the small shares, however, the effect on the loss ratio is considerably reduced. If, on the other hand, there were several ceding companies on both lists, the effect would be more serious, particularly due to a large windstorm loss.

Attaining an Equitable Match

Obviously, the probability of two insurers identically matching all of the above requirements is remote. As a result, certain methods have been utilized in an attempt to arrive at a sound and equiable compromise. If the disparity is too great, an equitable balance cannot be obtained, and an exchange of treaties cannot be accomplished. Since the object is an exchange, a compromise can provide the answer. Adjustments can be made by increasing or decreasing (1) the commission or profit commission given or received, and (2) the percentage share ceded or received.

Individual consideration of these alternatives should give the reader an idea as to how they are properly applied. Should the liability exchange not be equal, the reinsurance commission may be adjusted to give the insurer accepting greater liability a larger share of the premiums ceded. Often, the commissions are left equal and a profit commission given to the insurer ceding the larger liability. The purpose of the profit commission is to furnish greater incentive for the ceding company to maximize the treaty profitability.

The other method widely used is that of changing the size of the shares ceded or assumed in order to balance premium volume and/or profit between the two shares. For example, assume Company A's 0.5 percent share has an estimated premium income of $10,000 and has experienced a five percent profit over the last five years or an expected profit on the share of $500. Company B's 0.5 percent share has an estimated premium income of $10,000 and has experienced a 2.5 percent profit over the last five years. Thus, in order to bring gross profits into line, Company B has to cede a one percent share to show a profit of $500 to match Company A's $500 profit, if the MPL of the one percent share does not increase Company A's hazard of accumulation to any degree.

CHOOSING PARTNERS

The careful selection of the ceding company by the professional reinsurer is an essential part of the successful reinsurance operation. This applies with even greater emphasis to the reciprocal reinsurer. Not only does the primary insurer have to utilize the normal section standards, but it also has to keep in mind that these may be competitors. Consequently, of utmost importance is the first standard which should be met by any prospective partner in reciprocity: the experience, quality, and integrity of management must be beyond reproach. Other standards which should be considered are (2) areas of operation, (3) general underwriting policies, (4) limits of retention in relation to premium income, and (5) past experience.

The implications of a ceding company having management whose integrity, experience and sound judgment have led it through a successful period of operation are self-evident. The importance of the prospective partner having these qualities has become even greater due to the streamlining of the treaty system. The reinsurer is becoming more and more dependent upon the ceding company for the successful conduct of its operations. This extends even further in the case of reciprocity. It must be recognized by each party that continuity, the fact of renewal, is necessary in order to allow the true function of reciprocity to be realized. The function of reciprocity is the counter-balancing of good and bad experience in any one year between reciprocal reinsurers so as to level out experience over the long run. Therefore, it must be determined that the prospective partner realizes that continuity is of prime importance.

The geographical areas in which the primary insurer actively writes business is also a major concern. The chance of accumulation is greater if the areas are mutually shared or if the proposing insurer already has bilateral reinsurers in the area. The accumulation hazard should be underwritten in a manner similar to the methods discussed earlier, and the size of the shares exchanged should be kept as small as possible.

The prospective reciprocal reinsurer's general underwriting policy is of obvious importance. Most insurers have their own ideas as to exactly what these policies should be. It may be generally stated, however, that the ceding company which is known to have conservative underwriting standards may be expected to yield reinsurance cessions which will be of the highest quality.

As the underwriting policies become less conservative, other factors become increasingly more important. The limits of retention must be carefully investigated to ensure that the reinsurer is not being selected against. The rule of thumb is the comparison between the ceding company's estimated net premium income to maximum possible loss and the same measure for the reinsurer's proposed share. These should yield ratios which are roughly comparable. If, for example, the insurer's ratio is thirteen to one while the ratio on the proposed share of the reciprocal treaty is five to one, a closer look at the situation is warranted. The prospective reciprocal reinsurer may be scrapping off more profit than is in the best interests of its reinsurers.

The results which can be expected under the treaty are not only reflected in the above ratios but also in the past experience of the treaty. Normally, the past five years are considered as the most applicable; anything more than that is essentially history and will have no real affect on the expected experience. If the last year or so reveals poor experience, the experience for the last ten years should be requested in order to indicate whether this was just an unexpected bad year or if the trend in results indicated that it could have been expected. Other items to look for if bad experience occurred are (1) a recent revision in underwriting policy, (2) introduction of a new area of coverage, and (3) general industry experience during that year. Often a definite factor or two can be isolated as the cause of the bad results, and action can be taken by the ceding company in order to correct the deviation. Corrective action should be taken before an exchange is consumated.

RAPID EVALUATION OF AN OFFER

The necessity of having some system of rapidly evaluating an offer of reciprocity is self-evident. Many hours of costly investigation and negotiation can be avoided on unsatisfactory offers. A method generally recognized as yielding a rough estimate of the desirability of an offer for treaty reinsurance, whether for reciprocity or otherwise, calls for consideration of four factors: (1) the last five years' experience; (2) the ratio of estimated premium income to MPL (maximum possible loss) for the share offered; (3) the proposer's approach to underwriter's estimate of PML (probable maximum loss); and (4) the growth of the premium volume under the treaty.

The importance of the past experience is evident. The items to consider when looking initially at the statistics are (1) volume, (2) loss ratio, (3) expense ratio, and (4) profit, both as a percentage and as a dollar volume. These should be compared to the same figures for the share to be exchanged.

The ratio of the estimated premium income to the MPL for the interest offered is of distinct importance and is easy to figure. This ratio reveals the balance of the treaty and should be generally around ten to one or better. The greater the ratio, the better is the balance of the treaty, and the more desirable it becomes to possible reinsurers.

A distinction should be made between the PML and the MPL used in insurance and reinsurance, respectively. First, in direct business, PML is used to indicate the probable maximum loss of a risk and is stated as a percentage, e.g., a wooden frame house will have an estimated PML of one hundred percent, whereas a brick house may have an estimated probable maximum loss of sixty percent. It is upon this estimate that the rate and retention are determined. Secondly, MPL is used in reinsurance to indicate maximum possible loss for a share of a particular treaty and is expressed as a dollar amount. This figure is calculated by deducting the retention for the best class of risk to be reinsured under the treaty from the maximum underwriting limit for that class. The figure so obtained is divided by the percentage share offered of the treaty to yield the maximum possible loss for the share. For example, Company A's net retention for Class A risks is $10,000, and the maximum gross line or underwriting limit is $100,000 for this class of risk; the maximum possible loss in this instance would be $9,000 for a ten percent share. Maximum possible loss is expressed as a dollar amount, whereas probable maximum loss is expressed as a percentage.

The third factor, the proposer's approach to probable maximum loss, is relatively easy to establish and is an important variable acting upon the treaty experience. The primary underwriter bases part of his decision as whether to accept a proposal of insurance, what rate to charge, and what the retention should be, upon the estimated PML. If the underwriting policy is a conservative one (e.g., no estimate of PML lower than twenty-five percent), the reinsurer can be assured that in all likelihood a reasonable line will be accepted. If a PML estimate as low as five percent is acceptable, the reinsurer should be sure that the other factors in considering the exchange are quite favorable. They may balance out the inadequate rates and larger lines which are set for the better risks. An attitude of "nothing lower than a PML of ten percent" is borderline, and anything below that is considered an indication of a poor moral hazard on the part of the ceding company.

The rate of growth of the premium income is an indication of the quality of the reinsurer's management. A steady growth of six to ten percent for an established insurer is considered to be optimum. Conversely, an erratic rate of increase or large increases compared to previous growth might indicate unstable underwriting policy. These are danger signals to the reinsuring underwriter, for such characteristics are often associated with poor management. A steady increase is normally the desired trend as far as the reinsurer is concerned.

The consideration of the four factors is a simple process which can be quickly accomplished. If not furnished with the proposal, the necessary information to perform this evaluation should be requested immediately to allow quick evaluation and tactful declination if such action is warranted. Table XII, Reciprocal Treaty Evaluation Worksheet, is included as a specimen form which may be used in setting down the evaluation information for easy comparison.

SUMMARY

Reciprocity is not a game for the uninformed. Distinct reinsurance underwriting policies have to be followed in order to realize profitable results. The first decision is the line of business to use as the basis of the treaty to be reciprocally reinsured. The basic characteristics for the "ideal" line are that the practices associated with it are widely recognized, the basic policy is relatively simple covering one or a few hazards, and the past experience is relatively stable.

After the basic line has been selected and the treaty established, the insurer should adhere to the rules of the reciprocity game: (1) The treaty must attain a wide geographical spread. (2) In order to minimize the effects of accumulation, the treaty should be split into small shares. These shares should not yield less than $15,000 in annual premium income. (3) The treaty accepted should be well balanced. (4) The original policies should be matched as closely as possible to ensure that an equal amount of risk is being assumed under each policy. (5) The treaty wordings should also be matched in order to allow for equal coverage in the agreement and give neither party any advantage within the agreement itself.

An important success ingredient in reciprocity is how carefully the reciprocal reinsurers are selected. The partners must be chosen carefully by requiring that they meet certain minimum standards. These standards include (1) the management's experience, quality and integrity, (2) its areas of operation, (3) the balance of each share, (4) the general underwriting policies, and (5) the experience for the last five years.

The reciprocal reinsurer must be able to separate the undesirable offers from the desirable ones with a minimum of effort and time. One method of quickly determining the desirability of an offer is to ex-

Table XII

RECIPROCAL TREATY EVALUATION WORKSHEET

I. Treaty Experience:

YEAR	VOLUME PROP.[A]	VOLUME OURS[B]	L.R. PROP.	L.R. OURS	PROFIT PROP.		PROFIT OURS	
19____	$____	$____	____%	____%	____%	$____	____%	$____
19____	$____	$____	____%	____%	____%	$____	____%	$____
19____	$____	$____	____%	____%	____%	$____	____%	$____
19____	$____	$____	____%	____%	____%	$____	____%	$____
19____	$____	$____	____%	____%	____%	$____	____%	$____

II. Maximum Possible Loss to Treaty – Proposed $____
Ours $____

III. Maximum Acceptable Underwriting Risk PML – Prosposed ____%
Ours ____%

IV. Average Premium Growth of Treaty – Proposed ____%
Ours ____%

Remember: Premium income divided by Maximum Possible Loss under the treaty *must* not be less than 1.0.

[A] Total Volume of Proposed Treaty
[B] Total Volume of Our Treaty

amine the following factors: (1) the last five years' experience; (2) the underwriting policy as regards the probable maximum loss estimate; (3) the balance of the share offered; and (4) the rate of growth in premium volume of the treaty. A quick perusal of these areas to ensure that they are favorable will enable the executive to accurately eliminate those offers which are most likely to yield unsatisfactory results.

Appendix A

Specimen Reinsurance Contracts

APPENDIX A

SPECIMEN FIRST SURPLUS FIRE TREATY

REINSURANCE AGREEMENT

between

(HEREINAFTER REFERRED TO AS
THE CEDING COMPANY)

AND

(HEREINAFTER REFERRED TO AS
THE REINSURER)

ARTICLE I

The CEDING COMPANY hereby binds itself obligatorily to cede and the REINSURER binds itself obligatorily to accept a fixed share of .... percent of the CEDING COMPANY's First Surplus, being all those surpluses over and above the amount retained by the CEDING COMPANY for its own account on all insurances, whether accepted direct or by way of reinsurance, against the risk of fire or against any other peril which may be insured through the fire department of the CEDING COMPANY situated within the United States, and the District of Columbia; provided that the share so ceded shall not exceed .... percent of the amount retained by the CEDING COMPANY for its own account.

The CEDING COMPANY may reinsure elsewhere a part or the whole of the insurances or reinsurances that normally would come under the scope of this Treaty, should this appear to be in the interest of the REINSURER.

ARTICLE II

The following perils, risks, and kinds of insurance are excluded under this agreement:

1. Inland Marine Business, also bridges and tunnels.
2. Ocean Marine Business.
3. Hulls (Ship Bottoms).
4. Automobile Business (other than Vehicle Property Damage under Extended Coverage Endorsements attached to Fire Policies).
5. Growing Crops.
6. Aircraft and Aviation risks (other than Aircraft Property Damage under Extended Coverage Endorsements attached to Fire Policies).
7. Flood, Rain, Frost and Freeze, Hail (unless included under Extended Coverage Endorsements attached to Fire Policies).
8. Water Damage (other than Sprinkler Leakage or as covered under Extended Coverage Endorsements attached to Fire Policies).

9. Excess of Loss Covers of every description granted to other insurance companies.
10. War Risk of any kind, direct or indirect, or Fire and/or Explosion however caused by foregoing, as excluded under a Standard Policy containing a Standard War Exclusion clause.
11. Earthquake liability when unaccompanied by or in excess of Fire liability on the identical risk.
12. Steam Railroad Syndicate business (exclusive of fixed properties and specifically rated risks).
13. Factory Insurance Association Business.
14. Underwriters Grain Association Business.
15. Oil Insurance Association Business.
16. Cotton Insurance Association.
17. All risks which are commonly known as Target Risks, including the following:

George Washington Bridge
A/C Port of New York Authority

Holland Tunnel.
A/C Port of New York Authority

Lincoln Tunnel (Midtown Tunnel).
A/C Port of New York Authority

San Francisco Oakland Bay Bridge.
A/C California Toll Bridge Authority

Golden Gate Bridge.
A/C Golden Gate Bridge and Highway District

Bronx-Whitestone Bridge.
A/C Triborough Bridge and Tunnel Authority,
New York, New York

Queens Midtown Tunnel.
A/C Triborough Bridge and Tunnel Authority,
New York, New York

Mississippi River Bridge at New Orleans, (otherwise known as the Huey P. Long Bridge).
A/C Public Belt Railroad Commission of the City of New Orleans

Tacoma Narrows Bridge.
A/C Washington Toll Bridge Authority, Washington
Use and Occupancy of whole Triborough Bridge structure.
A/C Triborough Bridge and Tunnel Authority,
New York, New York

Brooklyn Battery Tunnel.
A/C Triborough Bridge and Tunnel Authority,
New York, New York

Chesapeake Bay Bridge.
A/C Baltimore National Bank, Trustee, State of Maryland and State Roads Commission as their respective interests may appear

Article III

The liability of the REINSURER hereunder shall commence and expire simultaneously with that of the CEDING COMPANY, as soon as the retention of the CEDING COMPANY on one risk is exceeded. All business hereunder will be ceded on the Policies Attaching Basis.

The CEDING COMPANY shall have absolute discretion in fixing the amount of its retention on any one risk and in determining what constitutes one risk.

If a loss should occur after the CEDING COMPANY has become liable on a certain risk but prior to the time that the CEDING COMPANY in the regular course of business has had an opportunity to place reinsurance on said risk, the CEDING COMPANY shall fix its net retention and shall cede to the REINSURER its portion of the First Surplus just as if no loss had occurred.

If the total amount accepted by the CEDING COMPANY on any one risk exceeds the limits prescribed by the CEDING COMPANY in its instructions to its branches or agents, the REINSURER shall nevertheless be responsible for its share of such excess but so that its share of any risk shall not exceed the proportion of the CEDING COMPANY's retention set out in ARTICLE I hereof.

Article IV

THE REINSURER agrees to follow the fortunes of the CEDING COMPANY in all respects as if being a party to the underlying insurances or reinsurances.

Errors, accidental omissions or oversights shall not prejudice the CEDING COMPANY, but any such error or omission shall be rectified as soon as discovered.

All books, registers and documents relating to this Treaty shall at all reasonable times be open to inspection by an authorized representative of the REINSURER.

Article V

The CEDING COMPANY shall pay to the REINSURER its proportion of the same rate of premium the CEDING COMPANY receives on the original insurances (subject only to the deductions of such discounts, brokerages, and commissions, taxes, or other amounts as are required by governmental regulation or local custom which the CEDING COMPANY itself has to pay).

The premium deduction which the REINSURER makes to the CEDING COMPANY on the business transacted hereunder includes provision for all Federal, State and other premium taxes, all board, exchange, and other assessments, and any other expenses whatsoever, excepting loss adjustment expenses. The CEDING COMPANY undertakes and agrees to make reports on the business transacted under this agreement to the various states wherein it may do business and any municipalities therein where it is required to pay premium taxes or assessments imposed by law or by the ruling of supervising officials. In the event, however, of the REINSURER being obliged to pay premium taxes to the Federal Government or any state or municipality or to the insurance departments thereof on the premiums recevied under this agreement, such premium taxes shall be refunded by the CEDING COMPANY to the REINSURER, provided, however, that the CEDING COMPANY shall not in any case be required to pay taxes twice upon the same premiums.

Article VI

The REINSURER shall pay to the CEDING COMPANY a commission of .... percent upon the net premiums, i.e., premiums, less returns, cancellations and deductions as credited to the REINSURER under this agreement. In addition, the REINSURER shall pay a profit commission of .... percent on the profits derived from this agreement and computed as follows:

To the credit account:
- The premium reserve (if any) from the previous year
- The reserve for outstanding losses (if any) from the previous year
- The net premiums of the current year.

To the debit account:
- The losses paid during the current year
- The commission on the net premiums of the current year
- Taxes, License Fees not recoverable from the insured
- The premium reserve of 40 percent of the net premiums of the current year.
- The reserve for losses outstanding at the end of the current year.

The balance of the account shall be the profit or loss for the current year.

The profit commission account shall be made up annually as at the 31st December in each year. The profit shall be based upon the average of the profit or loss for the current year and for the two preceding years. Whenever a share of this treaty is allotted to a new reinsurer, the profit commission during the first three years shall be based as follows:

At the end of the first year: on the profit of that year;
At the end of the second year: on one-half of the aggregate profit of the two years;
At the end of the third year: on one-third of the aggregate profit of the three years.

In the event of this agreement being cancelled, the profit commission account for the last year of the treaty shall be made up only after all the liabilities of the REINSURER hereunder shall have been ascertained and discharged.

Article VII

The CEDING COMPANY reserves to itself the sole right to settle losses whether by way of compromise, *ex gratia* payment or otherwise. All settlements shall be unconditionally binding on the REINSURER. The CEDING COMPANY may contest any claim and institute any action it thinks fit in relation to a claim, and the REINSURER shall be liable for its share of the claim and all costs and expenses incurred in connection therewith, but the REINSURER shall be entitled to its share of any salvages or recoveries relating to such claim.

Immediate notice shall be given by the CEDING COMPANY to the REINSURER of all losses of which the total amount to be borne by all the reinsurers participating in the treaty is estimated to exceed $........................ All other losses will be advised by quarterly reports, and an estimate of all outstanding losses falling under this agreement will be furnished by the CEDING COMPANY as of December 31st, of each year.

Whenever the proportion of a loss failing to be borne by the REINSURER amounts to $........................ or more, the REINSURER shall pay the amount due within fifteen days after application therefor has been made by the CEDING COMPANY. All other losses shall be debited in the quarterly reports.

Article VIII

The CEDING COMPANY shall render to the REINSURER statistical reports as follows:

Quarterly, as soon as practicable after the close of each calendar quarter:

a. Written premiums with original premiums by term and expiring years.
b. Cancelled premiums with original premiums, by term and expiring years.
c. Paid losses reduced by salvage.
d. Adjustment expenses.
e. Unearned premuims, all classes combined, computed by the use of monthly pro-rata fractions.
a. Net premiums by States for each annual statement class.
b. Paid losses (less salvages) by States for each annual statement class.
c. Loss adjustment expenses by States for each annual statement class.
d. Outstanding losses as of December 31st, for each annual statement class, by States.

Article IX

The accounts under the agreement shall be made up quarterly as of the 31st of March, the 30th of June, the 30th of September, and the 31st of December, in each year, and shall be rendered by the CEDING COMPANY to the REINSURER as soon as practicable thereafter.

The accounts shall be confirmed by the REINSURER within fifteen days after their receipt and the balance on either side shall be paid within fifteen days after receipt by the CEDING COMPANY of such confirmation.

Article X

This agreement shall take effect in respect of all insurances issued or renewed on and after the 1st of January, 19...., and is concluded for an indefinite period, unless either party shall terminate the agreement by giving three months' notice in writing by registered letter, such notice to expire on the 31st of December in any year.

Should the REINSURER at any time:

a. Lose the whole or any part of its paid-up capital
b. Go into liquidation whether voluntary or compulsory or suffer the appointment of a receiver
c. Amalgamate with or pass under the control of any other company or corporation

the CEDING COMPANY shall have the right to terminate this agreement forthwith at any time by giving notice in writing by registered letter to the REINSURER.

In the event of any law or regulation becoming operative which may prohibit or render illegal any part of the arrangements made under this agreement, the CEDING COMPANY may forthwith terminate this agreement so far as it relates to the business to which such law or regulation may apply.

This treaty shall also be terminable without previous notice in case any of the countries where the contracting parties are domiciled should be involved in war or be wholly or partly occupied by another power, in which case a portfolio withdrawal shall be effected.

Article XI

In the event of this agreement being terminated under paragraph 1, 2, and 3 or Article X hereof, the liability of the REINSURER under any cessions current at the date of the termination of this agreement shall continue in full force until their natural expiry, provided, however, that the CEDING COMPANY shall have the option to withdraw the portfolio of existing cessions as of the date of such termination.

In the event of the automatic termination of this agreement under paragraph 4 of Article X hereof, the CEDING COMPANY shall withdraw the portfolio of existing cessions as of the date of such termination.

Article XII

This agreement may at any time be altered by mutual consent of the parties either by addendum or by correspondence signed by a responsible official of the parties and such addendum or correspondence shall be binding on the parties and be deemed to be an integral part of this agreement.

Article XIII

In the event of the insolvency of the CEDING COMPANY, any reinsurance shall be payable by the REINSURER on the basis of the liability of the CEDING COMPANY under this agreement without diminution because of the insolvency of the CEDING COMPANY.

In the event of the insolvency of the CEDING COMPANY, the liquidator or receiver or statutory successor of the insolvent CEDING COMPANY shall give written notice of the pendency of a claim against the insolvent CEDING COMPANY on the policy reinsured within a reasonable time after such claim is filed in the insolvency proceeding. During the pendency of such claim, the assuming insurer may investigate such claim and interpose, at its own expense, in the proceeding where such claim is to be adjudicated any defense or defenses which it may deem available to the CEDING COMPANY or its liquidator or receiver or statutory successor. The expense thus incurred by the assuming insurer shall be chargeable subject to court approval against the insolvent CEDING COMPANY solely as a result of the defense undertaken by the REINSURER.

Where two or more REINSURERS are involved in the same claim and a majority in interest elect to interpose defense to such claim, the expense shall be apportioned in accordance with the terms of the reinsurance agreement as though such expense had been incurred by the CEDING COMPANY.

ARTICLE XIV

Any dispute or difference which may arise in respect of this Treaty or transactions hereunder, which cannot be settled amicably, shall be referred to a Court of Arbitration. Each party shall appoint its Arbitrator, and the two Arbitrators thus appointed shall appoint an Umpire. If either of the parties fails to apoint its Arbitrator within four weeks after the other has requested it by registered letter, or if the two Arbitrators fail to agree upon the Umpire, then the second Arbitrator and/or the Umpire shall be appointed by the Insurance Commissioner of the New York State Board of Insurance.

The Arbitrators and the Umpire shall be unbiased persons and must all be Presidents or Chairmen of insurance or reinsurance companies domiciled in the United States. The Arbitration shall take place in New York, New York. The Arbitrators are relieved from all judicial formalities and shall interpret this agreement from a practical view and from equity rather than in a strictly legal sense. The decision of the Arbitrators shall be taken within six months from the date of their nomination and shall be binding on the contracting parties. The costs of the Arbitration Proceedings shall be apportioned as decided by the Arbitrators.

This Arbitration Clause is an independent agreement between the parties and is in force, even if this Treaty Agreement in other parts should not be valid from the time of agreement. The Arbitrators are thus also entitled to decide in question of party's pleading against the validity of the Treaty Agreement as well as the consequences thereof.

In witness whereof, this agreement has been signed in duplicate on behalf of the contracting parties, each party receiving one copy:

In____________________this________________day of__________19_____.

____

(CEDING COMPANY)

Attest________________________________ By____________________

and in____________________this________________day of__________19_____.

____

(REINSURER)

Attest________________________________ By____________________

SPECIMEN EXCESS OF LOSS REINSURANCE CONTRACT

between

(HEREINAFTER REFERRED TO AS THE REINSURED) ON THE ONE PART

AND

(HEREINAFTER REFERRED TO AS THE REINSURERS) ON THE OTHER PART.

ARTICLE I

This agreement is to indemnify the REINSURED in accordance with the provisions and conditions herein contained in respect of all payments made by the REINSURED as a result of any loss or losses which may occur during the currency of this Agreement in respect of their net participation in all insurances, whether direct or by way of reinsurance (hereinafter referred to as the original insurances) accepted by the REINSURED situated at any part of the World but limited hereunder to:

I. Cargo and/or Merchandise and/or Interests underwritten in the REINSURED'S Cargo Account, whilst in transit in any vessel or ashore or afloat or airborne, but excluding:
   - (a) Hulls and/or Disbursements Premiums.
   - (b) All other Shipowners Interests, Ship repairers Liabilities, Drilling Risk Insurers.
   - (c) Overdue Risks.

II. Cotton and/or Cotton Seed and/or By or Related Products and/or Coffee and/or Boiler and Machinery and/or Interests underwritten in the REINSURED'S Fire Department.

ARTICLE II

Any loss or losses recoverable under this Agreement shall be subject to the undermentioned Clauses.

As regards the perils of tornado, cyclone, windstorm, hurricane or hail, the term "loss occurrence" shall mean all losses caused by tornadoes, cyclones, windstorms, hurricanes, or hail storms incurred during any continuous period arising from the same atmospheric disturbance.

As regards the peril of earthquake, the term "loss occurrence" shall mean all losses caused by earthquake incurred during any continuous period of seventy-two hours.

As regards the peril of riot, civil commotion and riot attending a strike the term "loss occurrence" shall mean all losses caused by riot, civil commotion, and riot attending a strike incurred during any continuous period of seventy-two hours.

As regards the perils of vandalism and malicious mischief, the term "loss occurrence" shall mean all losses caused by vandalism or malicious mischief incurred during any continuous period of twenty-four hours.

Excepting as above provided, the term "loss occurrence" shall mean one or more occurrences, disasters or casualties arising out of or following one event.

The REINSURED may elect the moment from which each of the above specified periods shall be deemed to have commenced, but such election shall not result in the inclusion of an individual loss under more than one loss occurrence as herein defined.

Article III

It is understood that where the original policy covers risks of War, Strikes, Riots and Civil Commotions it shall be subject to the current London and/or American War, Strikes, Riots and Civil Commotions Clauses, and such risks shall be subject to seven days notice of Cancellation at any time.

It is further understood that where a Riots and Strikes endorsement or corresponding endorsement approved by a Local Tariff Association is attached to the original policy this insurance shall follow the original in all respects.

Article IV

This agreement shall take effect at Noon on the thirty-first day of December, Nineteen Hundred and .... (Local Standard Time) at the location of the respective risks covered by this Agreement and shall continue in force for an indefinite period, but either party shall be at liberty to terminate this Agreement as of the anniversary date of any year by giving ninety days previous notice of cancellation in writing by registered letter.

Article V

No Claims are to be paid under this Agreement for any loss unless the REINSURED has paid or advanced to its insured on account of loss subject to any restriction which may be expressed in the special Clauses and Conditions herein, an amount exceeding U.S. $100,000 (one hundred thousand) ultimate net loss in respect of any one loss or series of losses arising out of the same event and the sum recoverable under this Agreement shall not exceed 100% (one hundred percent) of a further U.S. $1,000,000 (one million) ultimate net loss in respect of any one loss or series of losses arising out of the same event.

This Agreement shall at all times be subject to the following expressed warranties:

I. Warranted that the REINSURED retain minimum of $100,000 any one ultimate net loss for their nett Account.

II. The Export in respect of business falling under Article I Paragraph 2 shall limit their retention to a Maximum Possible Loss for the perils of fire to one million dollars.

III. The REINSURED shall limit their maximum retained line under Aritcle I Paragraph 1 to one million dollars any one ocean going vessel.

Notwithstanding anything to the contrary herein the REINSURED shall have the right if required of calling upon the REINSURERS hereon to settle any claim(s) recoverable hereunder simultaneously with the settlement(s) made by the REINSURED under their original policies or contracts of insurance.

Article VI

The term "*Ultimate Nett Loss*" shall mean the sum actually paid by the REINSURED in settlement of losses or liability after making deductions for all recoveries, all salvages, and all claims upon other renisurances, whether collected or not, and shall include all adjustment expenses arising from the settlement of claims other than the salaries of employees and the office expenses of the REINSURED.

All salvages, recoveries or payments recovered or received subsequent to a loss settlement under this Agreement shall be applied as if recovered or received prior to the aforementioned settlement and all necessary adjustments shall be made by the parties hereto. Provided always that nothing in this Clause shall be construed to mean that losses under this Agreement are not recoverable until the REINSURED's Ultimate Nett Loss has been ascertained.

Article VII

In the event of any of the liability hereunder being exhausted by loss, the amount so exhausted shall be automatically reinstated from the time of occurrence of the Loss without payment of an additional premium, subject to Limits of Liability set out in Article V.

Article VIII

All loss settlements made by the REINSURED, provided same are within the conditions of the original insurances and within the terms of the present Agreement shall be unconditionally binding upon the REINSURERS and amounts falling to the share of the REINSURERS shall be payable by them upon reasonable evidence of the amount paid and sufficient data to establish the equity of the claim being given by the REINSURED: it being understood and agreed, however, that all papers in possession of the REINSURED connected with the adjustment of said losses shall, at all reasonable times, within one year after adjustments have been effected be open to inspection in New York by a properly authorized delegate of the REINSURERS.

Article IX

This Agreement is negotiated through .... and ...., through whom all communications to and from REINSURERS are to be passed.

In the event of a claim arising hereunder, notice shall be given through the intermediary mentioned above as soon as practicable.

Article X

The Annual Premium for this Agreement shall be calculated at 2% (two percent) of the original gross net premium income of the REINSURED subject to an annual minimum premium of $40,000 hereunder.

The term original gross net premium income shall mean the original gross premium under business the subject matter of this Agreement, less return premiums, granted by the REINSURED under the original insurance, less the premium on outward reinsurance (if any) recoveries under which inure to REINSURERS benefit. A Deposit Premium of U.S. $30,000 shall be due on issuance of this Agreement and thereafter annually, payable in four equal quarterly installments.

Article XI

The premium under this Agreement shall be calculated on the premium received by the REINSURED converted to United States Dollars at the rates of exchange adopted by the REINSURED from time to time for purposes of its own accounts and the amounts recoverable for losses shall be calculated at the rates of exchange of the bills drawn upon or cheques drawn by the REINSURED in settlement of particular claims or, when the payment is dealt within any Branch Office or Agent's account, at the rate of exchange adopted by the REINSURED for such account.

Article XII

In the event of war arising between the United States of America and the Country in which the REINSURERS reside or have their principal offices or are incorporated, this Agreement shall be automatically terminated forthwith and the liability of the REINSURERS under current cessions shall cease as from the date of the outbreak of war.

Article XIII

Should at any time any individual REINSURER:-

1. Lose the whole or any part of its paid-up capital; or
2. Go into liquidation or a receiver be appointed; or
3. Be acquired or controlled by any other company or corporation, the REINSURED shall have the right to terminate their participation in this Agreement forthwith by giving notice in writing to the REINSURER.

Article XIV

REINSURERS hereby agree notwithstanding anything to the contrary herein that in the event of the insolvency of the REINSURED, this contract of reinsurance shall be so construed that the reinsurance shall be payable directly to the REINSURED or to its liquidator, receiver or statutory successor by the REINSURERS in the event of the insolvency of the REINSURED on the basis of the liability of the REINSURED under the contract or contracts reinsured without diminutation because of the insolvency of the REINSURED. It is further agreed that the liquidator, the receiver or the statutory successor of the REINSURED shall give written notice to the REINSURERS of the pendency of a claim against the REINSURED on the policy reinsured within a reasonable time after such claim is filed in the insolvency proceedings; that during the pendency of such claim the REINSURERS may investigate such claims and interpose at their own expense in the proceeding where such claim is to be adjudicated any defense or defenses which they may deem available to the REINSURED or its liquidator, receiver or statutory successor; that the expense thus incurred by the REINSURERS shall be chargeable subject to court approval against the REINSURED as part of the expenses of liquidation to the extent of a proportionate share of the benefit which may accrue to the REINSURED solely as a result of a defense undertaken by the REINSURERS.

Article XV

The REINSURED shall not be prejudiced by any inadvertent error or omission or oversight to cede what may rightly fall under this Agreement, or to do any of the acts or things provided by the terms thereof, it being the intention of this Agreement that the REINSURERS shall follow the fortunes of the REINSURED in all matters falling under the Agreement.

Article XVI

If this Agreement should expire whilst an occurrence or series of occurrences arising out of one event or disaster and/or conflagration covered hereunder is in progress, it is understood and agreed that, subject to the other conditions of this Agreement the REINSURERS hereon are responsible as if the entire loss or damage had occurred prior to the expiration of this Agreement.

Article XVII

All disputes or differences arising out of the Agreement shall be submitted to the decision of two Arbitrators, one to be appointed in writing by each of the parties. These two Arbitrators shall appoint in writing an Umpire before entering upon the reference and should the two Arbitrators fail to agree, then the matter in dispute shall be referred to the Umpire and the decision of the two Arbitrators or Umpire, as the case may be, shall be binding and final on both parties.

The Arbitrators and Umpire shall be managing officials of Insurance Companies and the seat of Arbitration shall be New York, New York.

In the event of one of the parties to this Agreement failing to nominate an Arbitrator within one month after arbitration is requested or in the event of the Arbitrators failing to nominate an Umpire within one month after their appointment as Arbitrators, then the Chairman for the time being of the National Bureau of Fire Underwriters, New York, shall nominate such Arbitrator and/or Umpire.

The Arbitrators or Umpire as the case may be shall not be bound by the strict rules of the law but shall settle any differences referred to them according to an equitable rather than a strictly legal interpretation of the provisions of this Agreement.

The Arbitrators or Umpire, as the case may be, shall award by whom, and in what manner, the costs of the Arbitration shall be paid.

IN WITNESS WHEREOF THE PARTIES HERETO APPEND THEIR RESPECTIVE SIGNATURES.
Made and Executed in Triplicate

For and on behalf of______________________________(REINSURED)

in________________this__________day of________19____

for and on behalf______________________________(REINSURER)

in__________this__________day of______________19____

Appendix B

The Programming Sequence, Statistics, and Exhibits

TABLE XIII

THE PROGRAMMING SEQUENCE

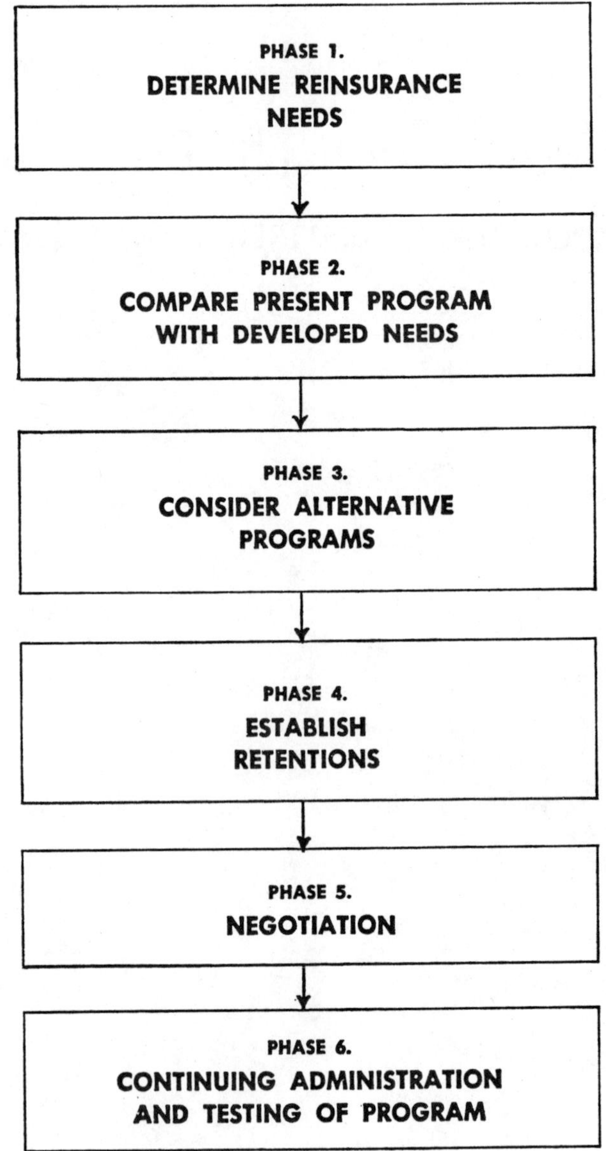

Table XIII
THE PROGRAMMING SEQUENCE
EXPLANATION

PHASE 1.

ANALYZE:

1. Line Sizes to determine "balance"
2. Geographical distribution of premiums. Fire, E.C., Hail, etc. to determine degree of catastrophe hazard
3. Coverage written
4. Premiums by line in relation to retentions

STATED UNDERWRITING SUPPORT REQUIRED OF REINSURANCE PROGRAM

1. Provide capacity
2. Stabilize loss ratio
3. Catastrophe protection
4. Protect surplus
5. Size homogeniety
6. Spread risk
7. Etc.

PHASE 2.

Determine How Well The Program Presently In Effect Satisfies The Stated Needs.

DISPLAYS:

1. Experience comparison with and without present program (working program, not catastrophe)
2. Net cost exhibit (net cost of each reinsurance agreement in effect)
3. Challenge support needs as stated in phase 1.

PHASE 3.

CONSIDER ALTERNATIVES:

1. No reinsurance
2. Different forms of reinsurance agreements
3. Reciprocity
4. Different retentions
5. Combination of above

DISPLAYS:

Same as phase 2.

PHASE 4.

ESTABLISH RETENTIONS WORKING PROGRAM:

1. Surplus & Quota Share
   a. Homogeneity
   b. Balance (Ratio of Estimated premium income to PML)
   c. Reciprocity
2. Exposed Excess – Displays:
   a. Variation in loss ratio
   b. Loss Frequency Experience per $1,000 of claims
   c. Integrated cost

CATASTROPHE PROGRAM

1. Maximum underwriting limit
2. Cushion theory
3. Simple vs. aggregating net retention
4. Upper limit

PHASE 5.

NEGOTIATION: Always compute net cost for each alternative offered by reinsurers. Net cost = Premiums – commissions – contingents – recoveries.

Compute a rate for excess coverages desired and compare to rates reinsurers offer.

If too much dispariety, consider: 1) Looking to another broker, or Reinsurer and/or 2) Restating retentions

PHASE 6.

CONTINUING ADMINISTRATION

– The program must be continually monitored. Did it do what it was supposed to do last year? What needs have changed? Has the market changed?

STATISTICS REQUIRED BY MAJOR LINE

General

1. Earned premiums–gross and net after reinsurance
2. Loss and loss expense paid, losses outstanding–gross and net after reinsurance
3. Excess premiums and excess reinsurance recoveries
   a. Working or class excess contracts
   b. Catastrophe excess
4. Number of losses exceeding various retentions (generally $1,000 units unless accurate analyzation dictates smaller units, or significantly larger ones).

Specific

5. Distribution of extended coverage premiums per state
6. Distribution of property specialty coverage premiums per state (earthquake, hail, turkey and chicken, cotton, etc.)
7. Assumed reinsurance premiums and losses by ceding companying.

NOTE: All figures should be for the last ten years.

NORMAL PROGRAMMING EXHIBITS

I. Experience Comparison – With and Without The Present Reinsurance Program

A. Exhibit by reinsurance agreement (Exhibit I)

B. Exhibit by major underwriting units; e.g., property, casualty, surety package, etc. (Exhibit II)

II. Net Cost Exhibit (All Reinsurance Agreements In Effect) (Exhibit III)

Net cost = reinsurance premiums – reinsurance commissions – reinsurance recoveries – contingent

III. Losses In Excess Of Various Levels – Retention Setting

A. Exhibit by major line (Exhibit IV)

B. Exhibit by loss accumulations (catastrophe) (Exhibit V)

C. Variation in loss ratio (See Table VIII, page 113)

D. Loss frequency experience per $1000 of claims (See Table IX, p. 114)

E. Integrated cost of reinsurance at varying levels of retention (See Table X, p. 115)

IV. Catastrophe Experience Summaries (Exhibit VI)

Displays cumulative premiums and losses for each layer of catastrophe protection.

Exhibit I

EXPERIENCE COMPARISON – BY REINSURANCE AGREEMENT
BEFORE AND AFTER REINSURANCE

YEAR	DIRECT EARNED	NET EARNED	DIRECT INCURRED	NET INCURRED	DIRECT LOSS RATIO	NET LOSS RATIO
1959	$ 12,061.	$ 2,714.	–0–	–0–	–0–	–0–
1960	227,020.	42,657.	$418,586.	$106,231.	184.5%	249.0 %
1961	196,555.	47,174.	91,645.	22,891.	46.6	48.7
1962	177,062.	35,113.	402,413.	101,422.	226.5	288.85
1963	197,061.	50,677.	25,469.	7,539.	12.9	14.88
TOTAL	$809,759.	$178,335.	$938,113.	$238,083.	115.9%	133.50%

EXHIBIT II

EXPERIENCE COMPARISON BY MAJOR UNDERWRITING UNIT BEFORE AND AFTER REINSURANCE

(figures in $,000's)

	WRITTEN NET PREMIUMS	NET PAID LOSSES	GROSS RATIO	NET RATIO	COST*	COST AS % OF GROSS WRIT. PREMS.
1963						
Co. A.	$114,134	$52,449				
Co. A1	+ 0	+ 0				
	$114,134	$52,449		45.95%		
Reins.	+ 6,520	+2,611			$1,498	1.24%
	$120,654	$55,060	45.64%			
1962						
Co. A	$111,190	$44,840				
Co. A1	— 4,905	+6,451				
	$106,285	$51,291		48.26%		
Reins.	+ 5,250	+1,215			$1,872	1.68%
	$111,535	$52,507	47.08%			
1961						
Co. A	$ 90,219	$42,726				
Co. A1	+ 10,024	+4,647				
	$100,243	$47,373		47.26%		
Reins.	+ 3,997	+1,594			$ 777	0.75%
	$104,241	$48,967	46.98%			
1960						
Co. A	$ 90,211	$39,428				
Co. A1	+10,023	+4,381				
	$100,234	$43,809		43.71%		
Reins.	+ 3,409	+1,360			$ 663	0.64%
	$103,643	$45,170	43.58%			
1959						
Co. A	$ 84,662	$34,516				
Co. A1	+ 8,220	+5,068				
	$ 92,882	$39,584		42.62%		
Reins.	+ 2,918	+ 879			$ 779	0.81%
	$ 95,800	$40,463	42.24%			

*Cost = reinsurance premium – reinsurance commission – contingent commission – reinsurance recoveries.

Exhibit III

NET COST EXHIBIT**
ALL REINSURANCE AGREEMENTS IN EFFECT

YEAR	1st surplus	2nd surplus	First Working Excess $450 XS $100*	Cost/$10,000
1957	$231,000	—$ 59,500	—$ 72,500	—$ 1,800
1958	$553,500	137,500	198,500	4,900
1959	135,000	24,500	155,000	3,880
1960	815,000	76,500	— 650,500	— 16,,060
1961	604,000	55,000	270,000	6,670
1962	— 93,000	157,500	— 294,000	— 7,260
1963	459,000	258,000		

	Second Working Excess $700 XS $550*	Cost/$10,000	First Catastrophe $2,000 XS $1,250*	Cost/$10,000
1957	$ 72,500	$ 400	$357,500	$ 2,380
1958	74,500	420	414,500	2,760
1959	77,500	430	266,500	2,660
1960	82,500	460	265,500	2,660
1961	73,500	410	— 516,000	— 5,160
1962	22,500	490	281,000	2,810
1963	104,500	580	316,500	3,160

	Second Catastrophe $2,000 XS $3,250*	Cost/$10,000	Third Catastrophe $1,500 XS $5,250*	Cost/$10,000
1957			$ 47,000	$ 350
1958	$ 31,000	$ 490	48,500	360
1959	50,500	800	50,000	370
1960	70,500	1,120	53,000	390
1961	73,500	1,160	47,000	350
1962	67,000	1,060	56,000	420
1963	68,500	1,090	65,000	490

*Figures in $,000's.

**Net cost = reinsurance premiums – reinsurance commission – reinsurance recoveries. These figures represent the cost of that portion of the covers assumed by the reinsurers. It does not include the portion retained by the ceding company.

EXHIBIT IV

RETENTION SETTING
PERCENT OF LOSSES IN EXCESS OF VARIOUS LEVELS
EXHIBIT BY MAJOR LINE

From 1957 to 8/30/64

RANGE	NUMBER	PERCENTAGE	SUB-TOTALS NUMBER	SUB-TOTALS PERCENTAGE
Less than $100	158	26.466%		
$101-200	90	15.075		
201-300	52	8.71	300	50.251%
$301-400	31	5.193%		
401-500	41	6.868		
501-600	17	2.848		
601-700	10	1.675		
701-800	12	2.010		
801-900	11	1.843		
901-1000	13	2.178	435	72.866%
$1001-1100	10	1.675%		
1101-1200	7	1.173		
1201-1300	7	1.173		
1301-1400	5	0.838		
1401-1500	7	1.173	471	78.898%
$1501-1600	5	0.383%		
1601-1700	3	0.503		
1701-1800	3	0.503		
1801-1900	2	0.335		
1901-2000	4	0.670	488	81.747%
$2001-3000	29	4.858%		
3001-4000	11	1.842		
4001-5000	14	2.345		
5001-6000	9	1.508		
6001-7000	3	0.503		
7001-8000	2	0.335		
8001-9000	5	0.838		
9001-10,000	2	0.335	563	94.311%
$10,001-15,000	5	0.838%		
15,001-20,000	1	0.168		
20,001-25,000	6	1.005		
25,001-30,000	3	0.502	578	96.824%
$30,000-1,000,000	19	3.182	597	100.006%

Exhibit V

RETENTION SETTING
LOSSES IN EXCESS OF $200,000
EXHIBIT BY LOSS ACCUMULATIONS

1954	1955	1956	1957	1958	1959
$1,833,454	$342,149	–0–	$506,080	–0–	$210,834
208,080	201,356				300,853
1,210,541	273,443				
	230,292				

1960	1961	1962	1963	9 Mos. 1964
$2,166,670	$2,947,767	$1,320,541	$242,152	$500,000 (Cleo)
	236,855	275,899	500,750	590,000 (Hilda)
	209,050	230,697	246,180	
		399,818		
		233,827		
		354,430		
		372,957		
		573,040		
		213,019		
		500,000		

	Subject Premiums Written	Earned
1954	$44,731,206	$42,954,657
1955	47,245,132	45,485,144
1956	50,910,603	48,672,925
1957	55,806,687	54,118,958
1958	57,468,160	54,792,787
1959	59,567,892	57,051,653
1960	63,327,793	62,169,431
1961	62,469,411	64,739,027
1962	67,608,553	68,292,615
1963	70,109,156	69,895,336
1964	72,212,432	71,992,197

Exhibit VI

CATASTROPHE EXPERIENCE SUMMARIES

SINCE INCEPTION

First Catastrophe

YEAR	PREMIUMS	LOSSES	CUMULATIVE PREMIUMS	CUMULATIVE LOSSES
1950	$105,853	$1,113,676	$ 105,853	$1,113,676
1951	194,469	—0—	300,323	1,113,676
1952	196,886	—0—	479,210	1,113,676
1953	203,284	—0—	700,494	1,113,676
1954	260,394	934,516	960,889	2,048,193
1955	285,521	—0—	1,246,411	2,048,193
1956	371,390	—0—	1,617,802	2,048,193
1957	357,664	—0—	1,975,466	2,048,193
1958	414,281	—0—	2,389,747	2,048,193
1959	266,484	—0—	2,656,232	2,048,193
1960	265,632	—0—	2,921,864	2,048,193
1961	397,701	830,550	3,319,565	2,978,743
1962	281,218	—0—	3,600,784	2,978,743
1963	316,381	—0—	3,917,166	2,978,743

SECOND CATASTROPHE	PREMIUMS	LOSSES	YEAR	THIRD CATASTROPHE PREMIUMS	LOSSES
1951	$ 52,020	—0—			
1952	53,332	—0—			
1953	55,821	—0—	1963	$32,528	—0—
1954	58,150	—0—	1954	31,311	—0—
1955	61,418	—0—	1955	39,685	—0—
1956	66,183	—0—	1956	42,764	—0—
1957	72,548	—0—	1957	46,877	—0—
1958	74,708	—0—	1958	48,273	—0—
1959	77,438	—0—	1959	50,037	—0—
1960	82,326	—0—	1960	53,195	—0—
1961	73,309	—0—	1961	46,765	—0—
1962	88,364	—0—	1962	56,098	—0—
1963	104,436	—0—	1963	65,542	—0—
TOTAL	$920,060	—0—		$513,081	—0—

Index

This book has been set in eight and ten point Jansen Linotype. Handset type is Bembo italic.